# out of war

## TRUE STORIES FROM THE FRONT LINES

### OF THE CHILDREN'S MOVEMENT FOR PEACE IN COLOMBIA

### SARA CAMERON

#### IN CONJUNCTION WITH UNICEF

SCHOLASTIC PRESS NEW YORK

## unicef
### United Nations Children's Fund

A UNICEF PUBLICATION TO CELEBRATE THE
U.N. SPECIAL SESSION ON CHILDREN — SEPTEMBER 2001.
UNICEF BELIEVES THAT ALL THE WORLD'S CHILDREN SHOULD
GROW TO ADULTHOOD IN HEALTH, PEACE, AND DIGNITY.

p. iii © UNICEF / HQ00-0795 / DONNA DECESARE

p. vi © UNICEF / HQ00-0793 / DONNA DECESARE

LIBRARY OF CONGRESS CATALOGING-IN-PUBLICATION DATA

Cameron, Sara (Sara J.)
Out of war : true stories from the frontlines of the Children's
Movement for Peace in Colombia / by Sara Cameron.—1st ed.
p. cm.
ISBN 0-439-29721-4
1. Movimiento de los Niños por la Paz (Colombia)—Juvenile
literature. 2. Children and violence—Colombia—Juvenile literature. 3. Children and war—Colombia—Juvenile literature.
[1. Violence—Colombia. 2. Colombia—History.]
HQ784.V55 C35 2001   305.23'09861—dc21    00-069605

10 9 8 7 6 5 4 3 2          01 02 03 04 05
Printed in the U. S. A.    37
First edition, September 2001

The text type was set in Weiss.
Book design by Marijka Kostiw

To all
children
who live
with
violence

—S.C.

# table of contents

# introduction

OUT OF WAR TELLS THE TRUE STORIES OF NINE YOUNG people who have experienced war and terrible violence, yet have chosen to work for peace. All of them are part of the Children's Movement for Peace in Colombia, which was nominated for a Nobel Peace Prize in 1998 — and every year since.

The stories in *Out of War* describe the struggles of these young people as they try to cope with some of the harshest tests of life: Juan Elias with the assassination of his father; Wilfrido with death threats; Maritza with violence at home and gang warfare on the streets; Farlis with massacres that are tearing her town apart.

Millions of children who live amidst war have similar experiences. The difference for these and thousands of other young Colombians is that they have refused to become a part of the violence themselves. Instead, they look for solutions that offer a way out of war, and in the process they have established an extraordinary movement.

The Colombian war has lasted more than forty years. It is a brutal conflict between many different armed groups who struggle for control over land and for power. All the armed groups have abused the rights of innocent people. About five thousand people are killed every year in the war and most of these are civilians. Massacres happen almost every week. Since 1985, more than two million people — one in twenty Colombians — have been forced to abandon their homes because of the war. And disappearances and kidnappings are widespread: In 1999 alone, more than three thousand people were kidnapped.

As deadly as the war is, even more people fall victim to the general violence of the society. Colombian cities have some of the worst murder rates in the world, due to the lack of justice and huge chasms between rich and poor, urban and rural populations.

The war expanded rapidly during the 1990s, fueled largely by illegal drug money — Colombia is the world's leading producer of cocaine. As displaced families poured into towns and cities, and kidnapping rates soared, the government and armed groups failed in their efforts to launch peace talks. Eventually, people tried to take peacemaking into their own hands.

By the mid-1990s, a peace network called Redepaz had brought hundreds of peace groups together in an effort to give greater power to the peace movement. And the Conciliation Commission, made up of important civic and religious leaders, had embarked on a series of peace talks with one of the guerrilla groups. This effort to launch peace talks was entirely separate from, and at the time much more successful than, any efforts by the government. Yet the peace movement as a whole was weak and divided into a patchwork of efforts — until the Children's Movement came along.

The Movement began with young people working in isolation, trying to make real contributions to peace, and it grew into a flood of millions clamoring for their rights to life and peace. It evolved without a formal structure — there is no official leadership and anyone under the age of eighteen, doing anything to improve the quality of life in a community affected by violence, is considered to be a member. The Movement's goal is very broad — to end the violence that is tearing Colombia apart, whether it is related to the war, to street violence, or to abuse inside the home. The Movement also strives to build unity among young people, across racial, economic, and geographic barriers — unity that many adult Colombians lack.

The Children's Movement strengthened and focused the peace efforts of adults and helped to launch the country on a path towards fresh peace talks. Most importantly, though, it has begun to lay the foundation for peace in communities, schools, and families, which is essential if any political solution is ever to succeed.

This inspiring story of the Movement is best told through the individual stories of these courageous young people. As a policy of the Children's Movement, armed groups responsible for acts of violence are never identified by name. And, for their safety and protection, the full names and identities of the young people involved are not revealed.

# Juan Elias — 18

## PEACE IS THE BEST REVENGE

MY FATHER WAS KILLED TWO WEEKS AFTER MY FIFTEENTH birthday. Some men walked into his office and shot him and my cousin, Luche, who was helping out as a receptionist. She was nineteen years old.

They laid the bodies in caskets in the living room of our house in Aguachica, a small town in northeast Colombia. Many people came to pay their respects but one morning I was in there alone. I stood looking at my father and Luche, side by side in their coffins, and I remember thinking, "Why *two* in my family? In plenty of families one person gets murdered, so why two in my family? And why my dad? *Why my dad!* And why Luche?"

Luche had never done anything to anyone. Neither had my dad. He was a good man. He gave his services as a dentist free to families who could not afford to pay. And Luche had hardly begun to live. She had wanted to become a doctor. That was why she was helping him at the office.

I was supposed to have been with them as well. That morning, as my father rushed to work, I ran after him, calling, "Let me come. There's no school today! I want to come."

But he looked at me and said, "You're not ready. I don't have time to wait."

He left without me. That is why I am alive.

I was already involved in peace activities before my father was killed. Only six weeks earlier, I had been at a meeting of children and adults from all over Colombia where we had decided to create the Children's Movement for Peace. At that meeting I had talked as if I knew all about the war and its impact on children. I thought I understood because Aguachica, where I lived, was in the thick of the conflict. There were battles in the streets during the night. I was often woken up by gunfire. When I went to school in the morning, I saw the evidence — the blood on the sidewalks, the bullet-riddled buildings. And I had seen the victims at the morgue, not far from my father's office.

I had talked about this with confidence, as if I knew what the war meant — but when my father was murdered, I was shattered not just by grief, but because then I *understood* the war. I knew what it felt like to want to fight. I realized that no matter how much you want peace, you take a step towards violence when the war hits you personally.

This is the same trap that has caught so many people in my country.

The war has been going on all my life and all my parents' lives as well. Not many Colombians can remember a time when there wasn't war somewhere in the country. But it was not always as fierce as it is today, when so many armed groups are fighting one another — guerrilla organizations and para-military groups and the army. Some people say they are fighting for the poor, but the poor have suffered more than anyone else in the war. I think that some people are also fighting for revenge, or for power, or because they feel they have no other choice. Some young people join the armed groups because their families are poor and they see no other way out.

For many years, people in Aguachica managed to stay out of the war. People fled here to escape violence in other parts of the country. They came from all over Colombia, from the plains in the east, the coastal provinces of the north, and from the mountains that dramatically divide our country. For years, people from these different cultures lived quite happily in Aguachica, sharing their different festivals, foods, and games.

My brother Andrés was born in 1976 and I in 1981. In many ways, our early childhood was idyllic and privileged. We spent the week living in a huge rambling mansion in Aguachica town, where my father had his dental practice, but every weekend we went to our farm about ten miles away. My father loved it there. He was a dentist by profession, but in his heart he was a farmer.

The farm covered thirty-one acres and had two rivers running through it, one close behind the house, the other about half a mile away. The land was rich and fertile. We grew tomatoes, plantain, papaya, oranges, avocados, and other fruits in such abundance that we gave most of the harvest away. My father loved horses and from dawn to dusk he would be out riding or working with Hugo the horse trainer.

As a child I was quite ill with hepatitis and my parents were always protective of me, but Andrés was tough and extroverted. He had a passion for survival games. We "raided" the garden for bananas, sneaked oil from the kitchen, and cooked the bananas "Indian style" over burning rocks. We made bows and arrows, and hunted pigeons that we plucked and roasted ourselves. Sometimes we played barefoot soccer in the street, or cops and robbers, or guerrillas and soldiers. On hot days we plunged into the huge tank used for washing clothes, along with the dogs, some toads, and all our friends.

In 1989, my aunt moved into our house with her four children. Luche was the oldest cousin and my mother's goddaughter. They were always very close, more like mother and daughter. Even with so many people living there, the house in Aguachica never felt crowded. It was so enormous there were still some rooms we hardly used. The living room was so big we sometimes pushed back all the furniture to play indoor soccer!

Living as we do now, in a very cramped apartment and often afraid of what will happen next, the size of that house seems incredible to me. So does the freedom of the life we had then.

For me, becoming aware of the war was the same as growing up. It was always there but for a long time it seemed like something that happened to other people. In 1990, it was suddenly right on our doorstep.

When I was eight years old, a man was shot and killed not far from our house. I saw his body lying in the street. A few days later, my cousins and I were playing in our yard when a bomb exploded less than a block away. The noise was deafening but none of us knew what it was. We stood there watching the bomb smoke curl into the air until our parents rushed out and pulled us into the house.

That year all our cattle were stolen, and men started showing up at the farm, demanding food, shelter, and money in return for their "protection" services. My father tried to turn them away but it was difficult. He paid one man the equivalent of about six thousand dollars in pesos just to leave us alone.

In December 1990, we had a Christmas party at the house in town and were singing carols when shooting started in the street outside. The next day, Andrés and I counted twenty-five holes in the walls of our house. On Christmas Day, we received a letter demanding payment of ten thousand dollars. A week later, another message gave instructions on how my mother was to go alone to a certain mango tree near a neighbor's property and leave the money there. A third letter warned that we had until January 12 to pay up, or we would "face the consequences."

My father told the police, who kept watch while my mother deposited the money as instructed. No one ever turned up to claim it.

A few weeks later, my mother realized she was being followed every time she left the house. Then her brother, who also lived in Aguachica, received an anonymous call warning that my mother should be "very careful." Finally, someone telephoned our house threatening to kidnap me. The caller even gave the name of the school I was attending, the Francisco José de Caldas School, a small private school in a middle-class neighborhood of Aguachica.

My mother rushed to the school, grabbed me and my brother, and brought us home. The next day my family fled from Aguachica for the first time. My father grudgingly went with us. He thought my mother was overreacting. Yet within a week another dentist from Aguachica, Oswaldo Pajaro, was shot dead on an isolated dirt road near the town.

We never knew who had been targeting us or why. We could guess that it was because our land was fertile and someone else wanted it, or because someone didn't like my father's ideas. But we didn't really know *why*.

Most families displaced by the war are desperately poor and have nowhere to go. They move into camps or into over-crowded rooms on the edge of large towns and cities. In those days my family was lucky since we still had money. We moved into a large, rented house in the pretty neighborhood of San Alonso in Bucaramanga, about eighty miles from Aguachica. I didn't mind Bucaramanga but my father never liked it. He was an important man in Aguachica, but Bucaramanga had more than four hundred thousand people, and he was lost. He said it was easy for young people to adapt and start over but it was too late for him. He tried to establish a new dental practice but it never went well. Soon he was spending four days a week working in Aguachica.

In November 1994, after two years away, we went back to Aguachica, leaving Andrés in Bucaramanga to finish his schooling. My father and I were especially happy to be home. He was confident that things were really beginning to im-prove but my mother was still afraid. She says now, "What I feared most became reality."

My father never believed he would be killed because he said he had never done anything to hurt anyone. It seemed much more likely that one of us would be kidnapped, especially me. We discussed how I should behave if this happened. I was to be respectful to any kidnappers, to answer their questions politely, to never try to escape, and to keep faith that I would soon be freed.

I began attending José María Campo Serrano secondary school in a quiet residential area on the outskirts of Aguachica. Dogs and donkeys wandered loose along the hot, dusty road leading to the school, which was set among mango, guayaba, and almond trees. The school was like an island of peace in the violent storm that raged in town. Every week something terrible happened. One weekend, ten teenagers were killed by the police after they tried to kidnap a farmer. Then almost the entire population of a nearby village, Patiño, was massacred.

After a massacre, people sometimes went to the morgue to see if anyone they knew had been killed. I went inside, just once. It is not something I want to describe. I was not afraid. It was just so sad. Many of those who died were young and had been tortured. Many people gossiped about the dead, and about what they must have done to deserve such a terrible fate.

"*Pueblo pequeno, infierno grande,*" my mother says now, which means "Small village, big hell."

Most people believed that the victims were guilty of something, but my brother and I realized this was not true when Edgar, a sixteen-year-old friend of ours, was tortured and murdered along with his uncle.

Towards the end of 1994, when I was thirteen years old, Luis Fernando Rincón was elected mayor of Aguachica and we were all hopeful that this would bring big changes. But days after Rincón took office, the director of the local hospital, Dr. José David Padilla, was murdered. Padilla was liked by many people and hundreds turned out to follow his coffin through the streets of Aguachica. A lot of us waved white handkerchiefs in protest against the raging violence. It seemed as if anyone who stood for peace and justice was at risk. They still are.

Soon afterwards, several armed groups informed Mayor Rincón that he was on their death lists. Rincón refused to be intimidated and instead announced that it was time for

Aguachica to take a stand against the war. He called together leaders in the town — doctors, teachers, business people, and my father as well — to discuss the situation. They decided to hold a peace referendum. A referendum is when people are asked to vote on a particular question. Our referendum asked: Do you reject violence and agree to convert Aguachica into a model municipality for peace? That was the dream Rincón had; that Aguachica would set an example for Colombia, and show how a town that had been so violent, could become peaceful.

The referendum was advertised on radio and television, in the newspapers and through public meetings and demonstrations. My father organized horseback rides for peace. More than forty of us, dressed in white, rode in processions through surrounding villages and Aguachica town. We were followed by the *papayera* who played folk music on wind instruments and drums, and by people carrying banners proclaiming Aguachica to be a "Model Municipality of Peace."

The whole atmosphere of Aguachica seemed to change and it certainly became less violent. More often I slept through the night, without being woken by gunfire.

I talked about the referendum with some students at my school and we decided that young people should also be allowed to take part in the vote. Through my father, I already knew the mayor so I volunteered to ask him. The mayor agreed and with help from his office, we launched a youth campaign that involved all the schools and youth groups in the town. We held ecological walks, dances, and peace marches. Up to eight hundred children from poor and middle-class neighborhoods took part in a massive "camp-out for peace" run by the Scouts. Hundreds came to peace concerts held in the San Roque Park in central Aguachica, where I introduced performers and sometimes played my guitar and sang peace songs.

Colombia had never had a referendum like this one, so many journalists came from the capital to cover the story. Some asked me for interviews, and my mother became worried because I started getting a lot of attention. Several priests who had been helping the youth campaign had already been threatened and forced to leave the town. My mother begged me to be careful about anything I said in public, and especially never to criticize anyone directly.

Becoming well known meant that some of the other kids

made fun of me. "Oh! Here comes the *pacifist!*" they would joke, "Here comes the *leader.*"

None of it bothered me. My family believed it was impor- tant to care about the community and to do whatever we could to help. Even though I was only thirteen, I could see that the biggest problems facing us were violence and the war. Peace was needed more than anything else. Of course it is hard for a child to try to make peace, but trying is the only way anything ever begins.

As the referendum grew closer, threats from the armed groups increased. Some of them announced that no one living in the mountain zones they controlled would be allowed to vote. They denounced the referendum as "no way to achieve peace" and said that all those who did vote would "have to suf- fer the consequences" because they would steal the list of vot- ers and take their revenge.

On August 27, 1995, almost 10,400 adults and about 4,000 young people voted to support peace while fewer than 50 voted against. We thought it was a big success, yet close to seventy percent of Aguachicans did not vote at all. Fear had stopped a lot of people from going to the polls.

For a while the violence in Aguachica calmed down but by the end of 1995, it was back again and just as fierce. More of those who had spoken out in favor of the referendum were forced to leave the town. Meanwhile, Mayor Rincón decided to appoint me as the Child Mayor of Aguachica, because of my work for peace. As the Child Mayor, I continued to visit schools to talk with students and teachers about creating a more peaceful and tolerant learning atmosphere. We held more youth concerts for peace, and organized a competition to see who could write the best peace song.

In May 1996, Mayor Rincón asked me if I would represent Aguachica at a workshop being organized by the United Nations Children's Fund (UNICEF). On May 23, 1996, I traveled to the meeting at the YMCA camp at Santandercito, just outside Bogotá. There were twenty-seven children and thirty adults at the workshop, all of them involved in working for peace, human rights, or with children in some of the most violent municipalities in the country. Fifteen-year-old Farlis, the Child Mayor of Apartadó,* was the oldest of the children. The youngest was nine-year-old Linía from Medellín. Other kids came from Cali, from the Guajira, from the Chocó, from

---

* See Farlis: The Line Between Now and Tomorrow

Bogotá, and many other places. None of us really knew why we were there and that first evening we were very shy and uncertain, hardly talking at all.

The workshop began the next morning with each of the young people describing their lives and activities for peace. Almost everyone started by saying, "My home is very beautiful" or "I love my home." We all felt that way. We talked about the people, the food, the parties and music, the oceans, rivers, and mountains, the heat of the sun or the cool breezes. Then we described the bad things, the violence and the way it affected children. I was amazed to learn it was just as bad for others as it was for us in Aguachica. I had heard news reports of the violence but I had not *realized* what it meant for so many Colombian children.

We also learned about other countries affected by war. Nidya Quiroz, who had organized the meeting for UNICEF, showed us a film about Mozambique, a war-torn country in Africa. The film covered an election in which nearly seventy thousand children had voted for their rights.

This led to a discussion of the rights of children. According to the law of almost every country in the world, children have a legal right to health, to food, to education, to play, to equality and nondiscrimination, to be protected from abuse, to express their opinions, to have access to information, and so on. In Colombia, of all places, we even had a right to peace! It was written in our Constitution and it applied not just to children, but to everyone.

On the second day, we young people were asked to recommend courses of action to oppose violence and promote peace and our rights. It wasn't easy. We soon fell into arguments and some of the adults found it hard to keep quiet. They kept saying, "But have you thought about this . . ." or "What about that . . ." They seemed to be putting pressure on us when really we needed time to work things out at our own pace. Finally one of the children, I forget who, proposed a vote to ask all the adults to leave the room. The motion was passed unanimously. Only Cynthia de Windt, who had organized the games we played at the start of the workshop, stayed.

It took us a long time to sort out our ideas but finally we were ready to invite the adults back in. We told them we wanted to create spaces where children's voices against the war could be heard, all over the country. We wanted cultural events where children could express their hopes and interest in peace through the arts. We wanted children all over Colombia to know about and understand their rights — and for parents and teachers to understand the rights of children as well. Finally, we asked the adults in the meeting to work as our partners in making these things happen.

Children and adults began working together to turn these ideas into a plan of action. In the middle of the third day, the Children's Movement for Peace was born. This was to be a real movement of children, which no adults could join. They could only be our advisors. The first activity of the Children's Movement for Peace was going to be an election, just like the one held in Mozambique, in which Colombian children would choose which of their rights were most important to themselves and their communities. The election would draw attention to the effect of war on children, but it would also help children, teachers, and parents learn about child rights. Before leaving, all of us signed a declaration agreeing to support the

Children's Movement for Peace and to promote the child rights election — which became known as the Children's Mandate for Peace and Rights.

I was so excited when I returned to Aguachica. A whole new way of seeing the future seemed to have opened up. I believed that if children from all over Colombia worked together we *could* change our country. Many people in Aguachica were discouraged by the renewed violence, but I kept talking about this new Children's Movement that was going to grow right across the country. I could see that what I was saying even gave some of the adults hope. They listened carefully and then, often, they would say, "I want to help you, tell me what I can do." They trusted me.

So many lies have been told in my country for so many years that people do not know what or who to believe any more. They cannot always trust the newspapers, the radio or television, the politicians, the armed groups — but when they hear children talking about the violence and the way it affects us and how we want peace, somehow they know they are hearing the truth.

Four weeks after I returned to Aguachica, our horse trainer,

Hugo, was murdered. Some armed men arrived at his house and set it on fire. As Hugo tried to rescue his daughter from the burning building, they grabbed him and forced his family to watch as they beat and tortured him. Hugo's fourteen-year-old nephew tried to stop the attackers. He ran forward shouting, "Stop! Please stop! Don't hurt him anymore!"

One of the armed men grabbed the boy and said, "So? You want some of this too, do you? You want some of this too?"

And they shot him. They killed the child and then they killed Hugo.

The surviving family members fled from the farm and for a while stayed in Aguachica town. Then they had to run away again. I don't know where they are now. They have been displaced by the violence like so many millions in my country. As I am too, now.

We always thought that Hugo's death and that of my father were connected, but to this day we have never been able to understand how.

In the next couple of weeks there were several signs that our family was in danger. One morning, my father and Andrés were held up and threatened on their way to the farm. We received sinister anonymous telephone calls, including one that warned my mother to take care of me. She was told, "A man with a gun has been asking questions about what time Juan Elias gets out of school."

Right away my mother contacted the army base next to the school to ask for protection. They told her that three army privates would be assigned as my bodyguards, but they never showed up so I did not go back to school.

About a week before the murder, my mother had a dream that she and the entire extended family were squeezed into my father's Renault. Everyone was there except him. We were traveling in a procession that was led by all the children. My cousin Luche, Andrés, and I were all dressed in white as if we were going to our first communion. Suddenly it began to pour, which was unusual. Aguachica is a very dry place. We rarely have big downpours.

My mother told my father about the dream, which she thought was a premonition of death, but my father never took such things seriously. He told her, "I am not ready to die yet."

The morning he was killed we had just driven up from the farm. The morning was already hot. The palms framing the entrance to the townhouse were wilting in the heat. We learned that his office had been trying to reach him, because some patients were waiting. One was a regular client. The others, we now believe, were the assassins.

We stood in the entrance to the emergency room, my mother closer to the door, and I about fifteen feet away, talking with Alexander, one of the human rights workers from Aguachica. He had come to the hospital as soon as he heard about my father. While we waited for news, many more people showed up, all wanting to know if it was true. I told many of them, "Don't worry. He's going to be fine. They're taking care of him."

I really believed it. Right after my dad was shot he had staggered out of his office calling for help. "I'm all right," he'd told one of his neighbors, "but get help for Luche!"

There were so many people waiting outside the emergency room that I did not see that the doctor had come to talk to my mother. A school friend of Luche's overheard their conversation and came pushing through the crowd towards me. "Juan Elias, your father just died," he said.

I thought it was a very sick joke. "Don't mess with me," I told him. "My dad is fine." But then I looked across the room, saw my mother's face, and knew it was true. I rushed to her.

My mother is a strong woman but I don't know what it was that ran in her blood that day. She had warned my father a thousand times about the danger he was in, but he wouldn't listen. Luche was still alive at that time but the doctor told us she needed a specialist's care. My mother found the strength from somewhere to call the army and try to get a helicopter to take Luche to the hospital in Bucaramanga. But the helicopter came too late and so Luche was taken there in an ambulance. The journey took much longer than it should have because a landslide had virtually blocked the road. Eventually, the ambulance managed to cross the landslide, but Luche died on the outskirts of the city.

My brother Andrés was already in Bucaramanga where he attended the military academy. We called him and told him to come home because our father and Luche had been killed. All day I had been very controlled but when Andrés walked into the house that evening it was as if a wall inside me broke down, and the flood rushed through. I fell on my brother and wept like a baby. Since then no one has seen me cry.

Nothing was the same afterwards. The house felt like a dead empty shell. The streets that were so familiar all looked strange. Nothing and nowhere felt safe. I thought all my work for peace was worth nothing because it had not saved my father. The horrific violence that had engulfed our town had finally struck the heart of my family — and I had been unable to stop it.

I blamed myself. I asked myself, "What had I done that my father should die in such a violent way?"

During the funeral it poured with rain, just as it had in my mother's dream. More than fifteen hundred bouquets were sent to us. The route to the church and the church itself were packed. My father had given so much to our town. He was loved by so many people.

The threats against my family continued even after my father's death. Every time my mother, Andrés, or myself left the house, we were followed. It felt too dangerous for me even to walk around the corner. I always traveled by car. My friends stopped seeing me. Partly this was because of their own fear but it was also my choice. I did not want to endanger anyone. Luche had been killed because she was with my father. I didn't want any of my friends to die just because they were with me.

I was frightened for myself and my family. I had only ever thought of how to make peace, not how to fight, but I was so afraid that I got a gun. I told myself that I would only use this gun as an absolute last resort, if I was in danger. But I was also angry. I thought, "If they try to kill me at least I will take some of them with me."

One evening, about ten days after my father was killed, my family and my aunt's family were gathered together in an upstairs room. I went downstairs to get something from the kitchen. The lower floor was in darkness and through the living room windows that overlooked the garden, I suddenly saw a shadow of a man. I ducked behind a pillar in the living room and watched him as he crept through the bushes. He was looking at the lighted windows upstairs. I could see the shape of a gun in his hand.

I realized that I could get my gun and kill this man. I could shoot him before he knew what had hit him. It would be revenge for my father's death. I would be protecting my family. And almost no one in Colombia would blame me for shooting him — violent revenge is the expected reaction of any young man who loses his father the way I lost mine. Yet while all of this was true, I did nothing.

My father had always wanted me to work for peace. How could I become violent now? The only way I could show respect and love for my father, the only way I could help to save my family, was by trying to make peace. The only way I could help ensure that no other child would suffer the way I had, was by trying to make peace. Killing him would bring no peace to me, or my family, or my country. In fact, by killing him I would lose everything. I would be no better than he was.

I watched him and then, for no clear reason, he turned and walked away. Not long afterwards I got rid of the gun and have never had one since. Two months later I went to Bogotá to take part in the first meetings of the Children's Movement for Peace. With all the grief I was feeling, it was a blessing to be able to throw myself into the Movement.

# Farlis — 19

## THE LINE BETWEEN NOW AND TOMORROW

WHEN MY COUSIN "ENRIQUE"* WAS SEVENTEEN, HIS GIRL-friend got pregnant. There was pressure to marry and he wanted to do the "right thing" anyway. He'd never attended school regularly and wasn't working at the time, but he went looking for a job to support his new wife and baby. He'd always dreamed of being a car mechanic but no one would take him on. He tried factories, shops, construction sites, and hotels. He tried all over our town of Apartadó, but he couldn't find a thing.

Eventually he decided he would have to join one of the armed groups. Some of the armed groups pay quite well, but the work is lousy. The work is all about killing.

Enrique and I are the same age and for years we have been very close. He is like my brother. When I heard that he was going to join one of these groups, I rushed over to his house and confronted him. He was in the tiny living room, stretched out in front of the television. I don't think I even said hello.

---

* Names changed to protect identities appear in quotation marks the first time they are used.

"How could you do this? How! I don't believe it!"

"Man, Farlis, I don't have no choice."

"You've always got a choice. There's always a choice, man!"

"I can't see it. There's nothing there for me. I tried every-where. How am I going to support my child?"

"You think *that* is the way to support a family? What kind of father would that make you? You call that a job!"

He looked away. "I don't have no choice," he said quietly.

"How can you even think of it!"

Did he think he would be able to kill? Would he be able to open fire on women and children and old people?

Certainly the men in those armed groups had money and power. They wore good clothes and expensive sunglasses. A poor young boy might easily think of it as a good opportunity, but only if he didn't think about the consequences.

"It doesn't come without a price," I told him. "There's a price to pay even inside this family."

He didn't look at me. He didn't speak.

"You listen to me. If you join up with them then you can say goodbye to me right now because you won't ever see me again or if you do then I won't know you, you understand?

Not only that, you won't ever see anyone in my family again. None of us. We won't see you. We won't talk to you. We won't know you."

I felt like crying. I loved Enrique but he couldn't do this! He still didn't look at me.

"You join up and that's the last you'll see of us," I said once more, and left.

A few days later I heard that he had changed his mind. Eventually he found employment on one of the banana plantations. It was low-paying and hard work, but it was peaceful.

I started working for peace when I was fifteen years old. By then I knew that this war is our war, it is my war. It does not belong to someone else, it belongs to me, to all Colombians. That is why I could not stand by and watch Enrique do this terrible thing.

The war has lasted so long because we have always waited for other people to make peace — yet no one else can do it for us. We must make peace ourselves. We cannot let another generation of Colombians grow up in the midst of war.

# # #

For fourteen years I lived on a banana plantation about ten miles from Apartadó, in the northwest region of Colombia known as Urabá. My father worked on the plantation, harvesting and packing bananas. My mother ran a small business from our home, selling soft drinks and snacks to the workers. We lived in a small adobe house with a tin roof in a dusty compound shaded by mango and guayaba trees. There were four kids in our family. I was the oldest, then came my brother Obier and sisters Elis and Yeleny.

We grew up rough, like other farm kids, playing in the fields, and swimming in the tank where they washed the bananas. We traveled to school hanging on to the back of a banana truck, bouncing over the rough roads, the air filled with the sweet scent of the fruit. It was hot and dusty and it didn't matter how much care we took before leaving home — by the time we got to school in Nuevo Colonía we always looked like farm kids.

Surviving in school meant being loyal to your friends and not being a *sapo*. *Sapo* literally means "toad" but it is also slang for an informer or a tattletale. We forced *sapos* to transfer to another class by ignoring them. It was harsh but it was also a reflection of the world outside. *Sapos* can get people killed in Colombia. Yet being unable to speak the truth — and sometimes all a *sapo* is doing is telling the truth — is a big problem too. There might be a massacre in the middle of a town in broad daylight but no one will admit to seeing anything. They will whisper the truth to one another, but they won't tell the authorities. They are too afraid.

When I was eleven, I was given the silent treatment myself, not because I'd been a *sapo*, but because I refused to take sides in an argument. A group of my friends had accused a girl in our class of stealing money and a huge conflict erupted. You had to be either for this girl, or against her, and all my friends were against her. Everyone assumed I would stand by them, but there was no evidence that the girl was a thief. I couldn't be sure. I didn't want to oppose my friends, though, so I just said nothing. Everyone got mad and, for a whole year, no one spoke to me.

Around that time my only friend, and the only one (I thought) who understood me, was a boy who worked on the plantation. We can call him "Alfredo."

The other farm girls teased me about him. They said, "You better watch out for that Alfredo, Farlis! You watch out girl because that boy is a *guerrillero!*" (a member of a left-wing armed group).

I knew some people around the plantation were involved in the war but I never thought that about Alfredo. He was too sweet and gentle. I thought the other girls were jealous because he was so good-looking.

Alfredo and I would walk for hours around the plantation, holding hands and talking about the future. I lay in bed at night imagining how Alfredo and I would marry and live together in Apartadó with our many children. But one day I walked into our house and found him there, cleaning his gun. He had come to buy something from my mother and, while waiting, had taken out his gun, and started to work on it. When I walked in, he gave me a smile, as if he were doing nothing out of the ordinary.

I have always hated violence, hated guns, hated the war. Alfredo tried to make excuses, the way people like that do, but I told him right away it was over between us.

"I don't want this kind of life for myself or for my children," I said. I was so young it seems like a joke now but I felt like my world was breaking in two.

Soon afterwards, Alfredo left the farm, but I was heartbroken. I couldn't sleep, my schoolwork suffered, and my mother was furious over my falling grades. I didn't know how to explain.

Finally my Spanish teacher, Señor Rodrigues, asked if I would like to "talk things over." We went to a small café in Nuevo Colonía and over some strong Colombian coffee I spilled the whole story of Alfredo, the gun, the silence of my friends, the teasing of the farm girls, my embarrassment, and broken heart. He seemed to understand everything. He didn't laugh at me, or make me feel young and ridiculous. He treated me like an adult.

"You must understand," he told me, "that you hold your own future in your own hands. Your future does not belong to anyone else, not to your parents, and especially not to this boy. It is yours and you can make of it anything you want."

After that, I didn't think of Señor Rodrigues as just my Spanish teachers, but as *mi profesor de alma*, the teacher of my soul.

# # #

One morning, when I was thirteen years old, my mother woke us up and told us that more than thirty people had been killed during an outdoor party in the old *barrio*, (neighborhood) of La Chinita in Apartadó. My grandmother, aunts, uncles, and cousins lived in *barrios* not far from La Chinita.

"They will all be fine," my mother told us. "I'll go there and see but they will all be fine." Yet there was fear in her eyes.

She went first to my aunt's house, then to my grandmother's, and then to La Chinita and the site of the massacre. The bodies were still lying in the street, their faces covered with cloths. People walked among them, lifting the cloths to see if anyone they knew had been killed. My family was safe, but a friend of my mother's was among the dead and my mother heard the story of how it had happened from one of the survivors.

There had been a party in the small plaza to raise funds for a local school. It was a beautiful evening and many people came out, young and old, to dance and have fun under the stars. Some of the people at the party were former members of one of the armed groups. Apparently they were the target of the attack, though most of the people who died were not connected with any armed group.

Around eleven at night, the party was in full swing when a truck full of masked, armed men drove into the square. They jumped from the vehicle and opened fire. They didn't seem to care who they hit. Old people and children were among the thirty-five people who died.

One of the men had drawn his gun on the husband of my mother's friend.

"Please don't kill him," she had pleaded. "Please, for the sake of our children, I beg you!"

But he killed them both.

After the massacre at La Chinita, the violence in and around Apartadó became much more intense. Armed groups sometimes turned up in villages, forced all the men, women, and children into the plaza, and sifted through them, executing anyone found guilty of supporting their rivals. They murdered grocers who sold food to the "wrong" side. They killed teachers who were teaching the "wrong" lessons. They slaughtered husbands in front of wives, parents in front of children, community leaders in front of entire villages. Many families were ordered to abandon their homes. Money was extorted from those they allowed to remain.

They sometimes showed up at farms like ours, gathered all the workers together, called out the names of supposed "subversives" and killed them. They also assassinated petty thieves and other delinquents, claiming that they were "cleaning up" the town. In the space of three years, more than twelve hundred people in Apartadó were assassinated, including seventeen members of the local government. Almost no one was arrested or brought to trial for these murders.

One of the worst massacres came in September 1995. A bus carrying workers from Apartadó to one of the plantations was forced off the road at a place called Bajo del Oso. They took the passengers off the bus, tied their hands, threw them face down in the mud, and opened fire. Twenty-five people died, including a fourteen-year-old boy. The few that survived only did so because they were protected by the bodies of the dead.

A friend of my father's was killed on that bus. We never spoke about it as a family, but we all sensed that next time it could be one of us. If my father was late coming home from work, we were all afraid but there was nothing we could do — or so I thought.

# # #

When I was fourteen, I began attending the José Celestino Mutis High School in Apartadó. During the week, I stayed with my aunt in the town. After the quietness and isolation of the plantation, I loved the energy of the town. Newspaper stories of Apartadó made it seem like everyone was allied with one armed group or another, perpetually plotting war or carrying out hideous acts of violence. In fact most people were never involved in the violence, except sometimes as its victims, and the violence wasn't continuous either. Most nights, the small bars of Apartadó blasted loud music, and people strolled the streets around the central park or sat at tables in sidewalk cafés.

I walked to school every day along the avenue beside the hospital. Teak trees grew close together along the roadside, their branches arching high over the road. Partway along this avenue was Don Fermin's fruit stall with its rich fragrances of papaya, mamocilla, mango, and banana. Don Fermin always called out a greeting as I passed, and if I missed a day at school he noticed and wanted to know the reason why. Many people in Apartadó were like him. They were sweet and caring and just happened to live in the middle of a war.

Celestino was tougher than my previous school, with a lot

of fights, petty theft, and drug abuse. Our ninth-grade class was considered to be the most disruptive in the school, but we were proud of this. We challenged our teachers and objected to the entire education system in Colombia, which favored the rich and privileged. We demanded more participation in deciding what and how we would learn. We verbally abused teachers who were inadequate, and I was often the ringleader of these attacks. I thought the school owed us a decent education. I thought that teachers who could not do their job properly had no business standing in front of the class. My desperation over my education grew as I grew. My parents were too poor to send me to university. I knew that whatever I learned at Celestino could determine my future.

My mother kept telling me not to worry. She promised everything would turn out well if I stayed true to my ideals. I love my mother very much and believe she is one of the wisest people in the world — but on this subject I thought she was crazy.

In 1996, when I was fifteen years old, one of my friends slipped my name onto the ballot for class representative.

I won that election and when all the student representatives got together, I was elected as the president of the student government. Then in April 1996, Gloria Cuartas, the mayor of Apartadó, invited several hundred student leaders to a special meeting. She told us that Graça Machel was going to visit Apartadó to learn about the effects of war on children.

These days, Graça Machel is better known as the wife of Nelson Mandela, but in 1996 she was studying the impact of armed conflict on children for the United Nations. For months she had been traveling from conflict to conflict, interviewing hundreds of people and gathering information for her report.

To prepare for her visit to Apartadó, more than five thousand children became involved in a Week of Reflection, which was supported by the Catholic Church, the Colombian Red Cross, and the United Nations Children's Fund (UNICEF). We wrote letters, poems, and stories, we painted pictures, and our work was posted on walls in the town hall.

One eleven-year-old girl wrote, "We know how to write the word 'peace' because our teachers have taught us which letters to use, but we do not know what it really means. It must be very beautiful."

Another child wrote an anonymous letter: "Dear Graça Machel, my father was the world to me, but since he was killed I cannot rest. I used to be a good student but now I only disappoint my mother. She tries to help but we live in the shadows, under a great weight of sadness."

The drawings were about the terrible violence of our lives. One picture entitled "My House" showed a simple dwelling, with a dead body lying in the foreground and presumably the family members gathered around.

"Violence in Urabá is stupid," wrote another child, "because we kill each other over stupid things. As the saying goes, *por ver caer*, to see is to die." He meant that if you witnessed a killing in Urabá, you were as good as dead yourself.

During that week, a hundred student representatives were divided into commissions to discuss different aspects of the conflict. There was a commission for peace, a commission for human rights, another for displaced people, and so on. We met in one vast hall in the Colegio Pueblo Nuevo in central Apartadó.

I was inspired by discussing and analyzing what had been happening to us, and by the idea that the views of children mattered. I remember telling our group in the Peace Commission, "People in Colombia would rather fight over a disagreement than talk about it. If they do talk, they are only interested in proving the other person wrong, not in finding common ground. But how can we learn to be peaceful if we don't understand what it means? No one here has ever lived in peace. We have been fighting from the time we were born and so have our parents."

By the end of the week we had plenty of ideas. We wanted peace education in our schools and a youth movement that worked for peace. We had also drawn up the Declaration of the Children of Apartadó, which asked the armed groups to stop killing our parents and to make the streets safe for us to play. We said that none of the armed groups had a role to play in the future of Apartadó but that the young people had a big role because we are the future.

Some towns in Colombia have Child Mayors who act as spokespeople for children. On the last day, I was elected the first Child Mayor of Apartadó. My first task was to present our Declaration to Graça Machel. I was fifteen years old.

The town hall was packed for her visit but I lost all fear when I went to the microphone. I said that people in Apartadó had been trying to forget the violence. They did not want to remember the terrible events of the war. Yet I was sure that for those who lost family members in massacres, like those of La Chinita and El Bajo del Oso, the pain would never die.

"If you kill the father, you always kill a part of his children as well," I said.

Then I read the Declaration aloud and presented it to Graça Machel. She promised she would carry our voices to the United Nations so that leaders from around the world would understand what the war was doing to us.

Things might have ended there but they didn't. We were inspired by that week. I was the Child Mayor and other students including Johemir* had also been elected to positions in a local government of children. We thought other students should know about their government and participate in it, so

* See Johemir: Journeys Far From Home

we sent out notices to all the schools inviting everyone to attend a meeting.

Truthfully, I thought that being the Child Mayor was a bit ridiculous. What could I really do? I had no power. I had no expectations about the first meeting either, but more than one hundred children showed up. When they kept on coming, to two or three meetings a week, I began to realize that we had really started something.

Most of us were between nine and fifteen years old. We met in parks or on soccer grounds, a rowdy mass of kids who argued ferociously about what we could and could not do to promote peace. We knew that ending poverty could help to end the war but we could do nothing about that. We knew that reducing unemployment would help, but we could do nothing about that either. We could not stop the bullets and the machetes. We could not end the violence. But we believed we could begin to build peace among ourselves.

My aunt lived in the *barrio* of Obrero and for several months that community had been feuding with the nearby *barrio* of Policarpa. It was difficult for young people from the two *barrios* to even walk through one another's territory. We planned a peace carnival for kids from these two communities where they could play together and see how much they had in common. With help from the Church, some of us visited parents in the two communities to explain the event. It was held on neutral ground, with water games and soccer, face painting, clowns, music, and more. Nothing like it had been seen in Apartadó before. It was a success but once was not enough. We planned more for the future.

We also organized youth clubs where the students could play music, basketball, and volleyball, or simply hang out after school. Yet any gathering of young people in Apartadó could be mistaken for a recruitment exercise for one of the armed groups. Just a suspicion like that could lead to violence, or even a massacre. As the Child Mayor I decided I should explain what we were doing to the commander of the most powerful armed group in the town.

Through another student I arranged to meet the commander — we can call him "Perez" — in a small café. He was a good-looking man, about twenty-six years old. He bought me a soda and seemed charming and interested while I explained that the school clubs would be "genuine youth activities." I told him that children in Apartadó needed to fill their minds and that this would help to take their thoughts away from the violence.

Perez told me these ideas were interesting. "We are here so that things will improve. I would rather young people were busy enjoying themselves than out joining the rebels or killing someone."

I had wanted to keep my meeting with Perez a secret because I was afraid people would think I was a sympathizer, but just talking with him established a connection between us. Afterwards, if I was in the street and he was passing, he stopped to talk. I was walking home from school with a group of friends one day, and Perez drove up with a truckload of armed men. He called me over and I couldn't ignore him.

My mother had told me that in life it is often necessary to be like a chameleon.

"Sometimes you must appear to be red even though you are green but no matter what you must always stay true to the essence of the creature that you really are."

I thought that in dealing with Perez I had to be a chameleon. I always kept my distance but I had to get along with him, because it was too dangerous to be his enemy. Not everyone understood.

Then Perez dropped by to speak with my mother. She was at home on the plantation, doing the family washing in a large cement sink on the back porch. Perez bought a soft drink and sat on a wooden bench nearby, chatting casually while she continued with the laundry.

He mentioned he had seen me on television and read stories about me in the newspapers. "So Farlis is becoming famous," he laughed. "What's all this about her becoming the Child Mayor of Apartadó? What does that mean?"

"It doesn't mean anything," my mother told him, "it's just something the children came up with. Children's rights. That sort of thing."

"Does she get paid for it then?" asked Perez.

"No, they're just kids. They don't get paid."

"She's young to get mixed up in politics," said Perez. "Doesn't it worry you?"

"It's not politics," my mother said. "It's the Church and the Red Cross. It's like a club."

My mother thought nothing of that visit from Perez but it

worried me. I knew that working for peace could be dangerous, and I was sensitive to anything that was out of the ordinary. Sometimes just the fear that anything bad could happen,
especially to my family, made me weep and feel like running
away from the peace movement. Yet the other kids were
depending on me, and in a way I felt that my own unborn children were depending on me too. I could not turn away, no
matter how afraid I was. I could only be careful and try to stay
safe.

Once a journalist tried to trick me into saying something
dangerous about one of the armed groups, just so he could get
a story. He would have sacrificed me for that. I learned never
to accuse anyone of anything — I would always describe atrocities and denounce the violence, but I never talked about who
was responsible. I simply said I did not know. This became a
way for all the young people in the peace movement to protect themselves.

A month after Graça Machel's visit, the Children's Movement
for Peace in Colombia was born during a workshop at Santandercito, just outside Bogotá. I returned from that meeting

full of enthusiasm. At the next gathering of the Apartadó movement, I told the kids, "Listen, we are going to make the whole of Colombia sit up and listen to us. There is going to be a special election for children called the Children's Mandate in which we will choose the rights that are most important to us. We have to make sure that every single child in Apartadó understands their rights and takes part in this vote. If we succeed then even the President, all the armed groups, and every adult in Colombia will have to listen."

It was a huge vision, this idea of making everyone listen to children. People were afraid for us. Some said that if children went to the polls to vote, they would become targets of the armed groups. For years every election in Colombia had been disrupted by violence. Eventually, even Cecilio Adorna, who led the UNICEF office in Bogotá, also began to have doubts.

UNICEF and a local peace organization called Redepaz were the main sponsors of the Children's Mandate. They had the backing of many other organizations, and about twenty young people like myself were advising on how to make it a success. Sometimes UNICEF flew me to Bogotá to take part in workshops and meetings. On one of these trips I heard that

Señor Adorna was thinking of canceling the entire election. Right away I went to his office and hovered beside his open door.

He looked up from his desk. "Farlis?"

"How can you do this to us?"

"Come in," he said, "sit down."

I sat and repeated myself. "How can you do this to us?"

"I am only thinking of your safety. The election could be very dangerous. They might harm you."

"But how can you disappoint so many children? They are looking forward to this. We have been working towards it for months."

"But what if a child is hurt? What then?"

"We have to take our chances. We can't let fear stop us. We have to trust that they will leave us to vote in peace."

I left it with him like that, and he spent a night thinking it over. The next day, the date of the Children's Mandate was set for October 25, 1996.

With UNICEF and Redepaz we wrote to the armed groups asking for peace on the day of our vote. Some of them even wrote back and told us they would respect our rights. One group even wrote about the rights of their own children, and about wanting to forge links between us.

The day of the vote came and for the first time in our memory there was peace, if only for a day, in Colombia. No child was hurt or even threatened. We had hoped that maybe 500,000 young people would take part but more than 2.7 million children and adolescents turned up at the polls. In some of the most violent towns, like Apartadó, almost every single person between the ages of seven and eighteen took part in the vote. Everywhere, children chose the right to life and the right to peace as the most important for themselves and their communities, and the most abused in Colombia.

I read the story of our election on the front page of our country's largest newspaper, *El Tiempo*. We were only children. We had no power, but we were making our country sit up and listen to us, because our ideas about the war and about the need for peace were important. I was amazed and happy and yet I knew it was only the beginning. A long struggle lay ahead.

## AFTER MILTON

I WAS EIGHT YEARS OLD, RUNNING ACROSS THE ROOF, WAVing my arms and screaming because the cat had a tiny bird pinned under her claws.

"No! Let go! Bad cat! No!"

The cat ran off and easily leaped to the next roof but I was moving fast, too fast. My foot caught on a loose stone. I tripped and fell off the roof and two stories down onto the dirt path below.

My skull was fractured. Everyone thought I would die. For days I was unconscious and then, when I did wake up, I could hardly speak or recognize anyone. I cannot remember anything from that time. The doctors wanted to give me a CAT scan, which is a special X ray of the brain. But it was expensive and my parents could not afford it. Just keeping me in the hospital for a few days took nearly all the money they had for the month. Yet even though people living in Soacha were poor, and even though we had lived there for only a short time, our

new friends and family found a way to help us. I got the treatment I needed and eventually I was healed. I remember coming home to tremendous warmth and love from everyone.

I think that is when I began to believe that there was no
problem we could not solve.


In January 1996, the day before Milton was killed, all the kids
from the neighborhood were out playing soccer. It was a
beautiful day and a great game. I was on Milton's team and
when we won, he grabbed me by the wrists and twirled me
around and around until I was screaming with laughter and
giddiness. He was fifteen. I was twelve and I adored him.

Everyone was so happy that day. It was such a long time
since we had all played together. Everyone was saying, "Oh,
we must do this again!"

Three days later we *were* all together again — only this
time it was for Milton's funeral and everyone was saying, "I
can't believe it!"

Around dawn, on the day after the soccer game, a gang
fight had broken out. Milton was at home but he heard the
commotion and went out to see what was going on. Milton

was a sweet person but lately he had been thinking about joining one of the gangs. He already wore the kind of baggy
clothes that gang members liked. When he went out to see the
fight that morning, he got dragged into it and they stabbed
him. When my sister Yeimi and I heard the news we rushed to
the hospital but they wouldn't let us see him. The doctor, confusing Milton with another boy, at first told us that he was
fine, that he had suffered only a small injury to his arm. Two
hours later the same doctor was explaining that he had made
a terrible mistake. Milton had been seriously injured and now
he was dead. Then Milton's mother came out of the hospital
and she was out of her mind because she had just seen his
body.

The wake was held in Milton's house, which is next to
ours. His body lay in a casket in the tiny room where his
mother usually slept. I am terrified of the dead but all night I
sat with Milton's coffin, sobbing uncontrollably until they had
to drag me away. When they tried to carry his coffin out of the
house I clung to it, because I couldn't stand to see him go.
When they buried him, I screamed "No! No!" because burying
him was like finally putting out the light of his life.

After the funeral, a group of us sat on the street corner near his house, crying and hugging one another and remembering how Milton used to tell jokes, make us laugh, and bring us gifts of little dolls and candy. All the time I kept imagining that any moment he would turn the corner and come walking towards us.

The next day we visited his grave and placed a vase of flowers in the niche. We visited Milton again the next day and again the day after that. Later, when we stopped going so frequently as a group, I began to visit him alone. It is nearly five years now since he died and I still go two or three times every month. I knock on the wall of his tomb to let him know I am there. I put fresh flowers in the vase, I look at his picture, and then I pray. Prayer takes me to a special place that I think no one understands unless they have been there; it is a place where I stand with God. Afterwards, no matter how terrible I have been feeling, or how depressed and angry, I feel much stronger and at peace.

I used to get angry about the way Milton died but I know it was not his fault, or even the fault of the boy who stuck the knife in his body. Milton died because of this war that rages on our streets and in our homes as well as in the mountains and forests. Since 1996, the year that Milton was killed, about five thousand people have been killed every year in the "war," and around twenty-four thousand have been murdered every year on the streets or in their homes.

The war is everywhere and if peace is ever to last we need peace everywhere. It was Milton's death that finally inspired me to work for peace, but I never imagined that it would carry me so far.

Soacha lies just outside the southern city limits of Bogotá. It is a rough and poor settlement with dirt roads and low cement houses. The land rises steeply and the higher up you go, the poorer the houses — some are made of no more than cardboard and plastic sheeting. Ten years ago few people lived here. We all arrived as squatters, seizing the land and making it our own. Most people came to escape the violence in other parts of the country, or like my family because they hoped that living close to the city of Bogotá would help them find a better life. But Soacha is a place of broken dreams and disillusionment. Most of us have stayed poor and the violence has not gone away either. People who live in the north of Bogotá are terrified of coming here. The north is where rich families live, in apartment buildings with security guards and elevators. They drive expensive cars, work in modern offices, take vacations in Miami, and go shopping in expensive malls. Soacha is an hour's drive away, down the *autopista del sur*, but for the people in the north it is like another country, an alien world.

Until I was seven years old I lived on a beautiful, small farm, about fifty miles south of Bogotá, with my family, my mother's parents, and many aunts, uncles, and cousins. The farm was close to an inactive volcano and the land was unstable. Landslides were common and the ground was always cracking open. Finally, about three years ago, a huge sinkhole opened and the entire house was swallowed up. No one was hurt, but several cows were also "eaten" by the earth. People living around there said that supernatural forces were responsible but I think it was the volcano.

By the time my maternal grandmother's house was swallowed by the earth, we were already living in Soacha with my father's mother. She and my uncle had built the house themselves. In those days it was made of wood and one of the supports was a tree that was still alive and growing. My family rented two rooms from my grandmother — one for my parents and the other for me and my sister. But it was hard for my father to find work and for a long time we had no money for rent. Eventually he became a bus-fare collector, but the pay was low, the work was irregular, and sometimes it was hard to find the money to put food on the table.

One evening, soon after our family moved to Soacha, Yeimi and I were out in the street playing "yermis" with some other kids on the block. Yermis is like tag except the chaser tries to hit the others with a ball. There was a small church near our house, and as we ran past, we noticed that the large metal door was open. My friend Monica looked inside and screamed because an enormous eye was projected on the back wall of the chapel. Right away we forgot about our game and crowded the doorway to see what was going on. That was how we met Sister Martha and Pastor Javier.

Martha invited us inside to watch the film (the enormous eye was part of the opening sequence). Afterwards she asked if we would like to meet with her on Saturdays, to play games and learn about God. There was nothing else for kids to do in Soacha, so we all said yes.

Martha and Javier worked with World Vision, which is a Christian organization that helps poor families in many countries. They give training to adults to help them earn money and to become better parents. They also provide a safe and fun place for children to go after school and on weekends. For three years we spent almost all our free time with Martha at what became known as the Timoteo Club. Our group of kids — which included Milton, Yeimi, Monica, myself, and other friends like Juan Carlos whom we knew as "Chiqui" — became child promoters. When Martha and Javier visited other communities to run workshops, we went with them to sing and play with the children.

Martha and Javier taught us that we could be leaders and help other kids who had problems like us. Another promoter named Harol, who came to Soacha in 1995, introduced us to the idea that children had rights. Having a place to live, food to eat, getting an education and health care, these were rights that belonged to all children, and not just to those who were rich. Harol also taught us that we had the right to express our opinions. He encouraged us to think and discuss the way we lived. He helped us believe we could change the way things were.

Soacha had become very violent. Armed gangs roamed the streets, attacking kids on their way to and from school, demanding money, stealing their pens and pencils, destroying their books, pushing the kids around, and sometimes worse. Some of these gangs claimed they "protected" the community, but they made life worse for many people. Some gangs came from the even poorer communities higher up the hillside. Some were just plain thieves.

Kids as young as eight or nine years old joined gangs because they thought it was cool or because they thought the gangs would give them protection on the street. In a lot of cases they were just trying to escape from violence at home, but they found something even worse on the street. Milton was not the only youth in our community to die in 1996. Two others on our block were killed in gang fights that year, and even more in the neighborhood. The violence was like an epidemic that was destroying us. It couldn't go on. I couldn't accept that this was going to be the life of our community, and do nothing about it.

In August 1996, we heard about the Children's Movement for Peace and, through World Vision, Monica and I became the elected representatives of the Soacha group. We regularly made the journey to the north of the city, to take part in workshops with young people from different parts of Colombia. I met Juan Elias, whose father had been murdered only weeks before, yet he was still working for peace. I met Farlis, who had helped to organize a children's movement in Apartadó. I had the chance to tell people about how we lived in Soacha. We exchanged ideas on the war and violence, on peacemaking, and child rights. Monica and I took these experiences back home, and shared them with anyone who would listen.

I started going into schools to talk with children about their rights and to encourage them to take part in the vote. Some were worried that they would not be able to vote because they had no identity cards. Either they had never been registered at birth or their papers had been lost when they fled from their homes. I talked about these problems with people from World Vision and UNICEF, and they made arrangements so that every child could vote, even those without papers.

On October 25, 1996, I rode in a bus with fifty other kids to the Plaza Bolívar in Bogotá to vote in the Children's Mandate. There were voting stations all over the city but the Plaza Bolívar is in the heart of Bogotá and thousands of children were planning to vote there. On the way, I stood in the aisle of the bus and invented peace songs. Everyone joined in.

We sang, "No to war, yes to peace because we the children are going to achieve it!" ("No a la guerra, sí a la paz porque los niños la vamos a lograr!")

The plaza was packed with children dressed in white, the color of peace. There were clowns and stilt walkers, people with peace doves painted on their faces, and people tossing white balloons into the air. Everyone was waving white handkerchiefs and hundreds of children were lined up at the voting booths.

I ran around the plaza shouting aloud, "Today, children are going to make peace in Colombia!" and attracted so much attention that several journalists from television and radio asked for interviews.

Eventually I took my place in the line, and voted for my right to life. By putting my mark on that ballot, I thought I was telling my country, "Listen, I exist and all of us realize what's going on. We care and we matter."

It felt so serious and yet I was happy because so many children were focused on the same idea: that we had the power to make peace. Even children as young as four or five years old wanted to vote, because they wanted peace.

The following day a group of us got together to watch the announcement of the results by the Registrar General on television. He was almost crying and we screamed when we heard just how many children had voted.

Many adults had supported the Mandate because they saw it as an educational exercise to help Colombian children learn about good citizenship. Instead, by voting in such huge numbers, and by showing that we really understood what the war was doing to us, we taught adults a lesson — they were the ones who had been letting us down. They were the ones who had not taken part in elections, had given us a weak government and had allowed the war to continue.

A month after the Children's Mandate, UNICEF, Redepaz, and the anti-kidnapping group called País Libre (Free Country) announced that they would support a Citizen's Mandate, to be held the following year. The Citizen's Mandate asked adult Colombians to support the Children's Mandate and to condemn the atrocities of the war — the kidnapping, disappearances, massacres, and forced displacement. It also asked for a ban on the recruitment of child soldiers by all the armed groups and for everyone to make a personal pledge to help peace.

Chiqui and I campaigned hard to get adults to vote in the Citizen's Mandate. Many had no idea that their own children had taken part in the Children's Mandate. A lot were skeptical.

"Why should we bother to vote? What difference can it make?"

"But look at the state of the country!" we told them. "Look what is happening! At least this is something you can do. You can be united and vote for peace."

On October 26, 1997, we went all over Soacha, urging people to vote, and when we heard the news that more than ten million Colombians supported the Citizen's Mandate, we were ecstatic. Now, none of the armed groups could say that they were acting on behalf of the Colombian people unless they were making peace.

Six months after the Citizen's Mandate, Andrés Pastrana was elected president of Colombia on a promise to make peace. Since then the government and the armed groups have begun to talk, yet despite this the war is worse. Every year, hundreds of thousands of people are forced out of their homes. More of them arrive in the city every day. The massacres and the kidnappings continue and more and more often children are the targets. We have made some important breakthroughs: the government agreed to end the recruitment of boys under the age of eighteen into the army. Yet the other armed groups continue to recruit children to fight. Often they put them in the front line, in the greatest danger.

Though the war continues, we can never give up. There is so much we can do, even right here at home.

Twice every week I go to different schools in Soacha or in even poorer *barrios* farther up the mountainside, like El Progresso, where those families who have most recently fled from their homes have settled. I have to take the bus to El Progresso but most of the bus drivers know about the work I am trying to do. They charge only what I can afford for the fare and often let me ride for free.

The road to El Progresso winds upwards, past rough shacks perched dangerously close to steep cliffs. The hills are deeply scarred where rocks have been removed for use in construction projects. Such work is hard, backbreaking, and poorly paid but many children from displaced families work on these sites. Their families have fallen into such deep poverty that the children drop out of school and do whatever they can to earn money.

From the road, I walk ankle deep in slippery mud, across a makeshift footbridge that spans a stinking, contaminated river. The school consists of half a dozen dilapidated rooms, clustered under a tin roof. The wooden desks are battered and broken. Rubbish litters the sides of the classrooms. There is no electricity. One of the classrooms has only a skylight and no other windows. The floor is made of dirt. The rain thunders so noisily on the roof that everyone has to shout to be heard, and water leaks through everywhere. One classroom wall is decorated with paintings done by the children, of pretty houses that contrast sharply with their surroundings. Perhaps these are images of the homes they once had or that they long for in the future.

There are no qualified teachers for schools like this so the government has sent police cadets to "teach" the children. The cadets have no training and run the classrooms in a military style that does not encourage much creativity or free expression. When I arrive the cadets hand the class over to me, and the children are usually very glad.

At first, when I ask a class "What rights do children have?" they often reply that we have the right to have a dog, to go to the park, to have friends, or to go swimming on Sundays. But then we talk about newborn babies and I ask, "What is the first right?"

"To life, to good health!"

"Doesn't this child get hungry and need something?"

"Yes," they answer, "the baby must have food!" And so we talk about the life of a growing child, and through this we discover all our rights.

I use pamphlets prepared by UNICEF and World Vision that explain the Children's Movement for Peace and the Convention on the Rights of the Child in simple language. The Convention is an international treaty of the United Nations, ratified by almost every country in the world (except the

United States and Somalia). I tell the kids, "Our rights are part of the law of our country."

Some of the children are withdrawn. Others are disruptive and want to draw attention to themselves. One boy called "Pepe" sometimes grabs the peace posters and tears them to shreds. Many have been traumatized by violence and the abrupt escape from their homes, but there are no psychologists around to help.

I met "Gladys" in El Progresso. She was fifteen years old and would often fight with the other kids. If we were working on an art project she would run around the room, upsetting the tables and spilling the paints. Gradually I learned what had happened to her family. They had been living on a small farm near Montería in Cordoba, but one of the armed groups had forced them to leave and they lost everything. Her father talked only of revenge and had banned her from taking part in any peace activities. Even though she was so disruptive, I could see she was interested in knowing more about the peace movement. So, one day, I persuaded Gladys to take me to her home.

The family was living in a one-room shack with no door. A piece of sacking hung in front of the entrance. Her father was home and I talked with him about the Children's Movement for Peace, and how we were trying to help children feel strong and capable of helping themselves. Later, I introduced him to some of the promoters from World Vision, and eventually he became a community leader himself. Sometimes Gladys is still disruptive, but she also talks to me directly now and often joins in activities.

Sometimes, a larger group of twenty or thirty young people in the Movement get together to run workshops for parents and children on family violence. World Vision provides the room and sends out invitations but we organize everything else. Children stand up in the meetings and talk directly to their parents about their experience at home. Then we discuss how parents can react in either violent or nonviolent ways when their children make mistakes.

Many of the parents have sadness in their faces. They talk aggressively to their children, calling them *"Chino hijuemadre"* (damn kid!) but during the workshops they sometimes begin to change. Some of them think they have to beat their children to make them behave, but then they realize that beating can also drive a child away and onto the streets.

Our friend Johanny used to write phrases for peace in his notebook and his father would get drunk and see them and rip them up. Then he would beat Johanny. One day Johanny wrote down a prayer for his father to stop hitting him. The father saw the prayer and he changed completely from that day.

I am now sixteen years old. My family still lives in two small rooms in Soacha and we are still very poor, but because of my work and experience I have traveled to many other countries. I have been to Europe, to America, to Panama and to Venezuela and even to New Zealand. People sometimes ask me: How can you do this? How can you cope with seeing how rich people live, staying in luxury hotels and then returning home to such poverty?

How can I cope? Because my home *is* my home and I have family and friends that I love very much. A hotel is only a hotel. The people we meet on the way are what really matters.

In the beginning, I only really cared about helping to improve things for people in Soacha. I know now that our problems here are connected to many others outside our community. I think that if we work to change things in Soacha we can stop our problems from spilling over into other communities. The same applies to Colombia. We have to deal with problems here to stop them from overflowing into other countries. When Farlis, Juan Elias, and I appeared on television in Panama, we said that the children in Colombia are struggling to make peace so that children in Panama will not have to suffer as we have.

A few years ago I had a recurring nightmare: I was running very fast and ahead of me was a huge cauldron filled with a boiling yellow liquid. I didn't know what the liquid was but I was about to throw myself into it. Then someone whom I recognized in the dream, but in reality I didn't know, grabbed me by the hand and wouldn't let me fall. He forced me to stop. Even now, I can remember every detail of his face.

At first this dream scared me because I was afraid that something very bad was going to happen to me. It doesn't frighten me now, perhaps because I believe there will always be someone there to help.

# Beto — 16

## FALLING IN LOVE WITH LIFE

EIGHTEEN MONTHS AGO MY ELDEST BROTHER "FREDY" showed up at our house in La Libertad, a poor community in Medellín. It was the middle of the night. He was drugged out of his mind and in deep distress. "They're going to kill me," he was murmuring. "I know they are going to kill me."

He wouldn't tell us what had happened, but there had been an argument between him and a gang in our neighborhood and now they were out to get him. He seemed full of grief and regret as well as fear that his days were numbered. He wanted to roll back time and make it better. He came to us because there was nowhere else to go, but he knew they would come looking for him at our house. He left that night and although we sometimes hear news of him, we haven't seen him since.

Fredy is my brother but he's like a stranger to me. When he was a baby my mother used to leave him with a friend of hers while she went to work. One day this "friend" — we can call her "Gloria" — told my mother that she wasn't going to give Fredy back. My mother begged and pleaded with Gloria and her family but they insulted her and told her she wasn't fit to be a mother. The police got involved but they didn't do anything. My mother tried to discuss things calmly, but Gloria's husband attacked her with a machete.

She didn't see Fredy again until three years ago. By then he was twenty-seven years old and messed up, into gangs, and taking drugs. He had a young daughter but he didn't treat her right. Some days he gave her everything she wanted. Other days he whipped her. He had no control over himself.

My mother lost Fredy long before I was born and I know it must have affected her badly. Maybe that was when she began to have a problem with alcohol. She never managed money well either. She had other children, some with one man and then with my father, but both of these men abandoned her. My older brothers and sisters did nothing to help. As they grew older, they started dragging her down. Everyone piled criticism on her, on each other, and on me as well.

I am the youngest in our family and for a long time I was at the bottom of this heap of suffering and violence. A lot of kids living in families like mine end up joining a gang or even fighting in the war. Most are looking for a way out of the pain they suffer at home, but they end up with something that is much worse. I managed to escape that fate because, despite all the sadness and violence in my home, I grew up feeling that I could get through it all and make a good life. I know my mother has problems, but I love and respect her. At last she is a good friend to me — but it wasn't always that way.

After she lost Fredy, my mother brought "Germán" to live in our house. I don't know where she found him but she adored him as if he were her own son. He was nine when I was born and was a menace to me when I was growing up. He always made me feel uneasy and insecure, and sometimes he hurt me. As a teenager he began stealing, first from us, and then from the neighbors. Eventually he was caught and when I was about eight years old Germán was sent to Bella Vista jail.

For a few years life was fine for us, but when I was ten, Germán came back. Prison had made him much worse and my life became a nightmare. He beat, tormented, and terrorized my sister Milena and me. We were never safe at home alone with him, but we didn't tell our mother what was happening. Germán threatened to beat us if we told and my mother seemed to love him so much that for a long time I didn't know if she would believe us.

At school I became a pest. I did anything to cause trouble. I messed around with cockroaches, shoved them in kids' faces. I called everyone names. The teacher with stuck-out teeth was "Crazy Fang." The math teacher's first name was Guillermo but I called him *"guerrillermo"* because it sounded like *"guerilla."* I talked in class, made silly noises that got everyone snickering, dropped books, or suddenly laughed out loud for no reason. I didn't care if a teacher or student was talking — I did anything to disrupt the class.

When my mother beat me, which happened often in those days, I screamed my lungs out. Afterwards I wrote messages to myself in a secret notebook — dramatic statements like:

"I am going to leave home! I know I can get on in life!"

Although I was so miserable at home and school, I always believed that someday everything would be okay. I don't know why, but I am known to be stubborn. Once I get an idea

I can hold onto it no matter what anyone says or does. I knew that running away wasn't the answer to my problems. Life was even tougher on the streets.

I found other ways to escape. Around that time a cartoon series called *Zodiac Knights* was playing on television. I played solitary fantasy games based on the show and always took the part of the heroic swan. The swan had fabulous feathers, bronze armor, and it moved with a powerful grace. Like him, I possessed incredible powers that I had acquired at the North Pole — the diamond dust that froze my enemies to death — and I defended Athens from the forces of evil. The swan's mother had died during a terrible shipwreck. In one dramatic game, I was about to be killed but, like the swan, I took out a rosary that my mother had given me, and thanked the gods for giving me such a wonderful mother. Because of that prayer the Cosmic Forces gave me strength to win the battle.

In the show, when the swan wanted to visit his mother's tomb, he had to crack the ice and dive into the depths of the cold, dark sea. I used to think, "I would do that for my mother."

But it was the Church that really gave me a way out of the violence at home. While Germán was in prison I had become an altar boy at the church of San Francisco de Assisi that lies on the border of the *barrios* of La Libertad and Caicedo. It was by far the grandest building in our community, soaring over the small cement houses, with a high arched doorway and a towering spire. Inside it was cool and dark. Light filtered through the narrow windows and lay in stripes across the pews, the altar, and the confession booths.

Ever since my first communion I had loved the rituals and the activity of the church. As an altar boy I helped the priests, handling the tray of wafers and the chalice during communion. I liked being part of the drama and the holiness of the place. The priests were also good to me, especially the Spanish priest called Manolo. He opened up a new world of ideas for me and always had time to listen, to talk, and to ask about my family. I worked hard to win his approval and to become the finest altar boy in the parish. Soon I was serving at every morning mass, as well as the Sunday evening mass.

By 1996, I was twelve years old and looking for every opportunity to get away from Germán. Through the church, I joined a theater and dance group that put on shows in the *barrio*. And through this group I heard about a workshop on community leadership. I went along thinking it would be for young people, but I turned out to be the only kid there. I didn't care. I hung around because I'm always curious and wanted to know what they were up to.

I just about fell over when they began to discuss violence in the home. It seems crazy but I never knew that people talked about things like that. I thought, "*¡¡Ave María!!*" because it was like coming to a place where people really understood what was happening to me.

I thought, "This is exactly what I have been looking for!" because these people also talked about how we could change things for ourselves. It was like the perfect glove slipping onto my hand! It never bothered me that I was only twelve and they were adults. I never thought, "Oh I can't do this because I am too young." I understood everything they were saying and knew right away that I could also be a community leader.

The workshop was run by an organization called Corporación Regional. Over the next few months I went to many more of their training sessions and often I was the youngest in the room by almost a decade. They liked me coming along. I was like their mascot. And, because of those sessions, I began to understand my mother better. I began to understand my own behavior at school better. Most of all I realized that I did not have to be a victim. Germán was still beating me up sometimes, but I finally realized that what he was doing to me was not my fault. I knew I could overcome it, and help other people do the same.

I tried to help Maritza*, who was also an altar girl at San Francisco de Assis. At first she wouldn't listen to me. She cursed me and said some terrible things. It was hard but I never let it stop me. Eventually we were able to close the gap between us, and to work together first through the church and then with kids in the community.

In June 1996, Alberto, who was one of the organizers of the Corporación Regional, called me urgently to the office. He introduced me to Oscar, who worked with the peace network called Redepaz. They were both very excited. Oscar told me, "There's going to be this amazing election for children about their rights! A Children's Movement for Peace has been formed! We've examined all our records and we've figured out that you should be the *procuradorcito* of Antioquia! It's great, huh?"

* See Maritza: One Foot in Violence, One Foot in Peace

I wasn't sure it was so great. A *"procurador"* is a lawyer or a solicitor who is concerned with civil law. *"Procuradorcito"* means "little lawyer" and Antioquia is the name of our province; a huge place with millions of people. Oscar was telling me that I should be the "little lawyer" of this huge province? It seemed ridiculous. Then Oscar introduced me to a boy called Gustavo Adolfo who he said was the *"alcaldecito"* ("little mayor"), to Harry who was the *"personerito"* ("little representative"), and a girl called Diana who was the designated *"consejerita"* ("little counselor."). He told us that the Children's Movement had the backing of some big organizations, and the first activity would be a child rights election called the Children's Mandate. The next day we went on local television to explain all this to other young people.

At first I was confused and thought they were manipulating me, but it began to make sense after we began teaching other kids about their rights. I worked in several schools in my own and other *barrios*. Groups of us ran recreational, theatrical, and artistic events to motivate the children to take part in the vote. Meanwhile, groups of *"semilleros"* (or "seedbeds" for

peace) sprang up all over the city. These were groups of children connected with the church or with human rights organizations; they worked together to promote child rights and
peace in their communities.

On the day of the Mandate, I went to the Campo Valdéz
school to cast my vote, and chose the right to life. Afterwards,
an argument broke out among several of us about which right
was most important. Harry had chosen the right to peace because he said there was no point in having a right to life if you
couldn't live in peace. Gustavo Adolfo had chosen the right to
justice because he said the lack of justice was the main reason
for the war.

But I told them, "What's the point in having a right to
peace or a right to justice if you're dead?"

I thought it was great that we had that kind of discussion.
It showed how seriously we took the election.

The turnout in Medellín was enormous. Almost every eli-
gible child voted. Afterwards, I thought, "What an amazing
thing to have done!" We even received a letter from one of the
armed groups telling us that they shared our dream of a coun-

try where everyone would be treated with equality and live in freedom. They invited us to visit and talk about our work, but we never replied or took up the offer.

Six weeks later I went to Bogotá to take part in the first Children's Assembly. I met Farlis, Juan Elias, Mayerly, and many other young people who were doing wonderful work for peace in their communities. It was a time of great hope — especially when the Citizen's Mandate also got such strong support — but after the Mandates, things in Medellín seemed to stall. We had no regular source of information about what was happening in the Children's Movement in other parts of the country so it was hard to keep that sense of unity.

I continued working in my church and community and gradually realized that the experience was changing me. I felt stronger and more confident. By the age of thirteen I had begun advising women in my community who were victims of domestic violence. The adult workshops of the Corporación Regional had given me information about the laws and organizations that protected and supported abused women. I passed this information on to one or two women in the *barrio* and they spread the word. Soon others were seeking me out, at the church, on the street, and at home. They trusted me at least partly because of my position as altar boy.

Many people in our neighborhood praised me and were grateful for the work I was doing, but at home I got nothing but criticism. Some of my relatives called me names and told me I was ignorant and weird because I spent time with young children. I tried not to let it affect me but it hurt that my own family didn't understand or value what I was doing.

In October 1998, I went back to Bogotá for the second Children's Assembly and I saw that the Movement was really expanding. I felt ashamed that we didn't have a better program organized in Medellín. John Fernando Mesa was also at that Assembly. He was a curator at a university in Medellín, and also worked with Redepaz. He also felt that Medellín should have a much stronger Children's Movement for Peace.

When we got back to the city, John Fernando, myself, and some other young people started working together. Through schools and youth organizations, we brought hundreds and then thousands more young people into the Movement. John Fernando established a base for the Children's Movement at the University of Antioquia in Medellín, where large numbers of kids from across the city would meet and talk about their experience and activities for peace. By 2000, more young people in Medellín were involved in some kind of community-based peace activity than probably anywhere else in the country. There still wasn't a lot of communication between all the groups, but we were making progress.

The Children's Movement for Peace was going well, but at home things with Germán were still difficult. Fights flared up out of nowhere. He destroyed our clothes, threatened us with knives, and sometimes beat me or my sister. He always won the fights.

One night when I was fifteen I was studying when Germán wanted to sleep. He told me to turn out the light. I refused so he turned it out himself. I turned it on again. He removed the lightbulb, so I found another lightbulb and fitted it. He stood over me as I was working, pushing me, and saying, "So, you really want me to stick the knife in, do you? You want me to stab you?"

Something snapped inside me. I stood up, grabbed hold of him, and threw him against the wall. I rarely lose my temper, but I lost control completely and hit him again and again. He pushed me aside and tried to grab a knife, and I got even madder. I seized a bottle and hit him. I hit him with anything and everything I could lay my hands on. I hit him for every time he had terrorized me and made my life a misery. I hit him for attacking me and my sister when we were too young and weak to protect ourselves. I hit him with every shred of power I possessed until my brother and sister pulled me away.

Most of the fight happened in the dark. When the light came on, no one could believe what I'd done to him. Germán was supposed to be the "tough guy." I was supposed to be the "weakling." That night it all changed. I know that since I am a peacemaker it should never have happened that way, but I was angry with him. I have never regretted what I did.

When my mother came home that night I told her everything, from beginning to end, all the things Germán had done to torment my sister and me, unspeakable things, and of course she was horrified. Of course she had never realized how bad it was. Of course she loved us and wanted to protect us, and right away she threw Germán out of our house. She tossed all his clothes into the street.

# # #

I should have talked to my mother sooner but when I was young I didn't know how to find the words, I didn't have the confidence, and I didn't trust her.

She doesn't understand how I grew up the way I did. She told me, "You used to be such a brat but look at you now! You are still a kid, but you think like an adult."

Recently, I noticed that she was becoming an alcoholic again. I don't mind if she has a drink now and then, but she was drinking every day, and too much of it. I waited until she was calm and sober, then asked her gently, "Mama, why are you drinking so much?"

"*¡Ave María!*" she sighed. "I'm bored. No one visits me. No one calls to say hello. Where are my children and grandchildren? I want to talk to them and have fun." They lived close by but hadn't spoken to her for ages.

I told she was crazy. "You kill yourself working for us all but you never complain. You just accept it. You should let them know how you feel."

"You don't understand," she told me. "You haven't had the experience I have had."

I could imagine her looking back over the tragic landscape of her life, beginning with the loss of Fredy. She'd lost that child three times over, once when Gloria's family took him, again when drugs took him, and again when he became a fugitive. The fathers of her children had abandoned her, and now her children were doing the same.

I said, "Well, I haven't had the same experience as you, but I've learned some things. I know that instead of spending your money on alcohol, you could buy a packet of *panela* [unrefined sugar cane] and some milk and bread. It would feed us a lot better than your drinking." But she just sighed. I wasn't getting through.

"Okay," I told her, "I'll join *you* then. I'm failing my ethics class at school. Instead of giving me any dinner, why don't you just go out and get me a nice bottle of *aguadiente* [a very potent alcohol] so I can drink it and then I'll be sure to pass my test tomorrow."

She laughed. "*¡Ave María!* it is better not to talk to you. You could shut up the Devil himself."

I help her with her money now. I also tried to speak to my

siblings, asked them to visit her, but it broke down into an argument. They still haven't come. I hope one day they will understand.

I am sixteen years old and have been in the peace movement since I was twelve. I run child rights groups in several elementary schools, training kids to teach other children about their rights. I believe that if children grow up knowing and respecting their rights, if parents, teachers, and all adults respect and protect the rights of children, then we will transform our communities. We could even end the war.

I also work with a group of adolescents in the nearby *barrio* of La Planta. Adults around here are frightened by any group of young people, which they assume must be a gang of thieves or murderers. We try to challenge that stereotype, for instance by organizing recreational activities for kids in the *barrio*. But it isn't easy because we have no funds and are working entirely on our own.

I've traveled to other countries to represent the Children's Movement for Peace, but I like Colombia better than any other place. It is tough here but life is rich as well. Overcoming the hard knocks, that is what makes you fall in love with life.

## ONE FOOT IN VIOLENCE, ONE FOOT IN PEACE

LAST SATURDAY I HAD A STRANGE FEELING THAT I WAS GOING to die. As I left the house, I told my mother "Don't wait up for me because I shall be killed tonight." She didn't say anything. My mother and I don't get along. It sounds pathetic to say "My mother doesn't love me" but I think this is the truth.

I went to meet my friend Fabio, who had just had a drastic haircut, very short, almost military. He gave me a rose and we laughed over it. We agreed that if either of us died that night then the one who survived would lay the rose on the other's corpse.

We walked up the hill from Caicedo, which is in the *communas* of Medellín. *Communas* means "communities," but in Medellín people use it to refer to the poorest and toughest neighborhoods. The heart of the city is beautiful and rich and lies in a valley. The *communas* crawl up the surrounding hillsides. The houses are packed close together, almost on top of each other, with narrow roads winding their way through. For fifty years people have been flooding into Medellín, trying to escape the violence in other parts of the country, but it seems they have brought the violence with them. Medellín has one of the highest murder rates of any city in the world. It has assassins and drug dealers, urban militias and gangs. You can live in the rich part of the Medellín and hardly get touched by any of this, but in the *communas* there is no escape.

That night, Fabio and I walked into the territory of La Libertad. At one time I could never have walked into that area because I used to belong to a gang known as "The Mexicans," who warred against the La Libertad gang. "The Mexicans" are finished now. Most of them are dead or else in prison. I am no longer a threat to anyone, but I still have a reputation. People know me. I've fired guns. I've been shot. I've done drugs. But I've also been a peacemaker. I walk two paths at the same time. I wish I could walk the peace path all the time, but something always gets in the way — my family, my community, my past, or maybe just being a girl.

That night, Fabio and I went into La Libertad because there was a dance in one of the garages up there. It only cost a thousand pesos (about fifty cents) to get in. The music was blasting and hard, the bass pounding so loud and low you felt it coming up through the ground, shaking your bones, your stomach, and your brain inside your skull. I love to dance and Fabio and I were out on the floor for a long time. Then he went off to the bathroom.

I was standing there, taking in the scene, when a huge guy lunged at me and shoved me up against the wall. He ripped my jacket off my shoulders, and pressed the barrel of a gun at the base of my throat.

"I'm going to kill you," he said. "I'm going to kill you because you are going out with a cop."

He was stoned. I could tell from his eyes and his voice. He thought Fabio was a cop because of his haircut.

"No," I told him, "I'm not going out with him and anyway he's not a cop."

The guy looked at me then grabbed my hand, opened my fingers, and pressed his gun into my palm.

"I want you to kill me," he said.

"Why should I kill you?" I asked.

"I want you to kill me so you know what it feels like to kill."

"Don't be stupid! Why should I kill you?"

"You think I'm joking!" he yelled.

Then he grabbed the gun, dragged me over to the door, and threw me out on the street. They grabbed Fabio and threw him out as well, then a whole crowd of those guys from the La Libertad gang were standing around us. They were all stoned or drunk or both. They said they were going to take us to different places and kill us. The atmosphere was as tight as a wire.

Lucky for us some other people from La Libertad came along — they are friends of mine and not part of any gang. I told them, "They want to kill us because they say that Fabio looks like a policeman."

They laughed and told the gang members, "Look at him. He doesn't look like a cop. We know him anyway, and he isn't one."

So they let us go. Fabio and I started walking down the hill towards Caicedo but a guy from the La Libertad gang was following us. It still wasn't safe. He could have jumped us at any time. I was glad when I saw another friend coming by on his motorbike. I flagged him down, Fabio and I squeezed on the back, and we rode home.

I have tried to make peace, even between gangs. Sometimes I think that no matter what we do, it will never be enough. The violence is so vast and insane. Maybe we can make a little progress towards peace one day, but it can all be destroyed the next. When I am with the peace movement and look at everything we are trying to do, I am easily discouraged. Yet when I stand in the middle of the violence, as I did that Saturday night, I know that making peace is our only hope.

I was the "surprise child" my mother never wanted. Her relationship with my dad broke up almost as soon as I was conceived. My mother soon got involved with my stepfather. I grew up thinking he was my real dad, until he got mad and told me the truth.

"And anyway, I'm not your real father!" he yelled at me. I cannot remember what the argument was about because that revelation cut through it like a knife.

My home was a battleground. There were, there are, fights every day. Everyone screamed and cursed. Whippings came for any reason. If I broke something — a cup, a plate, a glass —

my mother grabbed the electrical wire from the boom box and let me have it. Trying to explain had no effect. She thought the things I broke were more important than I was. I was always hungry as well. My mother and stepfather drank most of the money they got from working on the street.

By the time I was eleven, I'd had enough. I ran away and tried living on the street but that was even rougher and there was even less food. I went home and my mother gave me another beating for running away.

I was eleven when I first took drugs. At first I was terrified and guilt-stricken because I thought God was watching. Then I got high and stopped caring. Not long afterwards a girl told me that it was cool to carry a gun. She said it made people give you respect — and I was ready to do anything to have people respect me. She introduced me to "The Mexicans," who gave me a gun and taught me how to shoot. In return I stood lookout for them, and carried stuff for them when they were shifting locations. I was always ready to fight. I wanted to be tough. I never let being a girl stand in my way. It felt safer to be out on the street than to be at home. At home I couldn't protect myself.

One day my mother hit me so hard that my face swelled up. The principal of my school told me I should denounce her, and arranged for me to go to the family welfare department. The woman at family welfare said I had two choices. If I denounced my mother I would be sent away and would never see her again. My other choice was to go home and try to work things out. At first I said yes, that I would leave home forever, but then I had doubts. I didn't know where they would take me. I thought that since my mother had suffered a lot for me, I should stay with her.

I tried to patch things up with her. I dropped out of "The Mexicans" and stopped taking drugs — but it didn't last long. By the time I was twelve I was high nearly all the time, or else I was wiped out from the aftereffects.

One time when I was high I heard a gun battle break out. I had no idea who was fighting or why but I grabbed my gun and ran into the street. There were guys in the trees, on the ground, and dodging around the buildings, firing at one another. I dived onto the ground and tried to join in, except I had no bullets in my gun. It was stupid but I felt like I was in a movie. I was rolling in the dirt, firing the empty chamber, when I felt a sharp pain in my leg. I thought I must have cut myself on a stone, but my leg started throbbing and heating up. Blood was soaking through my jeans. I'd been shot! I left the battle and went home and showed my mother.

"That's what you get for not listening to me!" she yelled. "Didn't I tell you to stay off the street? Look at you!"

She hit me and said she wouldn't take me to the hospital. She thought that getting shot might teach me a lesson. I cleaned myself up. Fortunately the bullet had only grazed the skin.

I met Beto when he was eight years old and I was nine. He was an altar boy and I was an altar girl at the same church. All the time that I was hanging with "The Mexicans" I was still an altar girl.

I thought Beto was a geek. He was a skinny, small, weak-looking kid who talked too much. Over and over again I told him to go away and leave me alone. Curses just bounced off him. The next week he would be back again, talking and talking. He was always telling me that I was throwing my life away on drugs and violence. I couldn't believe it. I had a really hard reputation in that community and this skinny kid was always trying to give me advice.

When he was about twelve, Beto started working with some community organization. He had got together with a group of kids from the neighborhood and they hung out, to talk and play games. I saw them a few times, Beto and this group of little kids. It looked interesting but weird. No one our age did that kind of stuff.

"You should try it," he told me.

"Yeah right!" I said sarcastically. It looked good in a way, but I had a reputation to keep up. How could I do that if I was hanging out with some little kids?

A few weeks later he came back to me. "You're a good dancer. Why don't you teach them?"

He showed me a flyer for a dance competition that was to be held among the *semilleros*. *Semillero* means "seedbed" and was the name given to children involved in peace groups like Beto's that had sprung up in different parts of the city.

"I can't do that," I told him.

"Sure you can."

We arranged to meet the kids in the church hall. Of course

they knew me or had heard about me and right away I could see they were afraid. Everything about me — the clothes I wore, my hair, the way I spoke and the way I walked — everything said that I was from the other side. They clustered around Beto as if hoping he would save them.

"Don't worry," Beto told me. "Just start."

I put some music on the boombox and began moving around the floor. "Come on guys," I said. "Let's have some fun! Let's dance!" I was laughing at myself and the whole crazy scene in that church hall. The kids were watching and gradually moved away from Beto. They started laughing with me and moving with the music. Soon we were all on the floor together. It was a Saturday, in the middle of the day and I wasn't stoned. I was dancing with a bunch of eight- and nine-year-olds, teaching them my favorite moves. I really liked it.

I chose an old Michael Jackson track, "Bad," and choreographed a routine that showed two gangs who become friends through the music. Instead of confronting each other with weapons, they competed with their dance styles. The kids practiced hard and the whole routine turned out really well. We went down to the competition, and we won.

After the success of that routine I got the idea of trying it out for real, to have a "dance-off" between "The Mexicans" and the gang from La Libertad. "The Mexicans" agreed, so with the help of another friend, I wrote a letter to the La Libertad gang, inviting them to a dance competition. The letter was delivered by a neutral kid who lived between the two communities. To show they accepted the challenge, someone from La Libertad fired four gunshots into the air.

The dance-off was held on the football field of "The Mexicans." The field was one of the only flat pieces of land we had in our community. From there you could see across the crowded *communas* of Miraflores, Catalonia, and Pablo Escobar, named after the drug lord. Escobar had given about four hundred houses, health centers, and schools to that *communa*. Among a lot of people, he was a popular guy. He was eventually shot in a police raid.

At the time of the dance-off, I was fourteen years old. When the guys and girls from La Libertad walked onto our field, the atmosphere was tense and I was scared out of my mind. We watched them stroll over, the guys with that swaggering walk, their hands deep in their pockets. It was hard to tell what was going to happen. But the guys from "The Mexicans" stepped forward to greet them and they all hit high fives.

One of the La Libertad guys said, "Okay, let's get down." The huge sound system kicked in and hip-hop blasted out over the field. They must have been able to hear us all the way to the center of Medellín. There was a military base nearby and some of the soldiers came out to watch. Maybe that is why there was no trouble that day. A seventeen-year-old kid from La Libertad won the competition and nobody argued about it. We all agreed he was the best dancer.

I didn't have any hope that the dance-off would make permanent peace between the gangs, but I thought it was a start. Within two weeks it was clear we hadn't started anything. Some of "The Mexicans" murdered the twelve-year-old brother of one of the La Libertad gang members. They dragged the boy off a bus, tortured, and killed him, and after that open war was declared. By the time it was over nearly all "The Mexicans" were dead.

With that I stopped believing that the peace movement could do anything. I went to some of the meetings but I was easily bored. Sometimes I fooled around, pretending my hand was a gun, pretending to shoot people with it because something stupid like that could really upset them. It made me laugh, but Beto got annoyed. He said I had to make up my mind. Either I was in the peace movement or out of it. Fine, I told him, so I'm out.

I started hanging around with some rougher friends and doing drugs again. Sometimes I'd borrow a bicycle, take off on it, and not come back for a couple of days. My mother whipped me, then I'd fight her and fight my stepfather. It went on for maybe a year. I was miserable and afraid.

One day my mother beat me so hard she almost broke my arm. She was screaming at me and I was screaming back. I was in so much pain. I didn't care anymore, not about her, or me, or anything. I went into the kitchen and grabbed a bottle of something. I can't even remember what it was. I was crying and cursing, trying to open this bottle with my arm hurting so much. Finally I got the top off and took a gulp.

It was acid or bleach or something but I didn't swallow much of it. As soon as it touched my mouth, I screamed. My lips and tongue swelled up, my whole face expanded, my windpipe felt like it was closing up.

I don't remember much about what happened next but my mother took me to the hospital and they admitted me. They took care of my face, my mouth, and my arm. And they tried to persuade me to denounce my mother. I didn't. I felt too exhausted and too alone.

After she dropped me off at the hospital, my mother never visited me and neither did my stepfather. None of my friends came to see me either, except Beto. He came nearly every day and told me how things were going in the Children's Movement for Peace. He made me smile. Even those words, "the Children's Movement for Peace," helped me. They described a whole different world.

When I got out of hospital I stopped using drugs and went back into the peace movement. Beto was only fourteen but he was running child rights clubs in several elementary schools. I went along with him but I didn't feel comfortable working with such young kids. I wanted to work with young people like myself who were at risk of getting mixed up in gang violence.

I started going to workshops to learn more about the peace movement and realized that my experience of surviving family violence, gangs, and drugs — and even my small efforts to make peace — were valuable. I even spoke at big meetings, in front of hundreds of other young people.

John Fernando, a lecturer from the university, was the co-ordinator of the children's peace movement in Medellín. He asked a lot of questions about my situation. I didn't like it at first. I wasn't used to depending on anyone. I hadn't ever met an adult that I could trust. But John Fernando kept trying and arranged for me to move into a special institution for girls at risk.

The institution was run by nuns and was very strict. It was hard for me to adjust to all their rules. I always spoke my mind and the nuns complained that this caused trouble among the other girls. After a while they suggested I should go home. They promised to call me back, but they never did.

In February 2000 I went to Holland to represent the Children's Movement for Peace. It was like a dream to be in a place like that. We stayed in a good hotel and ate good food. Everywhere we went there were journalists, photographers, and television cameras. People kept telling us how great we were, because we were young people living in the middle of violence and trying to make peace.

I went to Holland with Juan Elias, who was a real front-runner in the Children's Movement. Like Beto he had been in it from the beginning and kept on working for peace even after his father was assassinated. He was a very middle-class kid but he was a good friend to me. He didn't care that I came from the *communas*.

The trip was organized by the Dutch Committee for UNICEF, who wanted us to talk to kids in schools about the Movement and the violence in Colombia. It was so hard to explain what our lives were really like. I was afraid to admit that no matter how much you try to make peace, you can still get dragged back into the violence.

When I came back from Holland, Beto and some of the others in the Movement thought I had changed. Beto said I was really full of myself. He didn't think traveling overseas was any big deal anyway. He'd been to Geneva with the Movement but he told me that "given a choice between Geneva and Cali, I would sooner go to Cali" — and Cali is just another Colombian city.

For me it was different because I have always longed to escape from this life. It is hard to admit but right now I am once again slipping away from the peace movement. I have been lying to myself and pretending to Beto and to John Fernando that everything is fine. This is not true. Sometimes I get high. Every night there are fights at home. If they are not yelling at me, my mother and stepfather are yelling at each other. I cannot stand it so I escape to the streets, and there is a lot out there that can do a young person harm.

I don't go to school anymore because I was attacked by some of the students and I am afraid to go back. I am seventeen years old but I have only reached grade eight. I can't get a job because I am under eighteen. Even when I turn eighteen it will be almost impossible to find anything. Unemployment is very high, especially among young people. And without a job there is no possibility of my moving away to live in a place where there is peace.

I walk two paths at the same time and still wish I could walk the peace path all the time. I think that my struggle to make peace and the way I have survived should be worth something. I would still like to help young people move away from gang violence, and perhaps make peace gangs instead. These would be groups of young people trying to help one another to survive the violence of their homes and the streets, without making life worse in the process. It is hard to do this without help. John Fernando helps but there are not enough people like him around.

I believe that young people would do a lot more to help peace if more adults were willing to cooperate, to listen to what we have learned and work with us. If we had peace at home, that would be a great beginning.

# Johemir — 16

## JOURNEYS FAR FROM HOME

IT TOOK WEEKS TO FIGURE OUT WHAT HAD HAPPENED TO Juanita. She couldn't tell it all at once. The story came out in pieces. Her mind kept wandering. Sometimes she cried so much we had to stop.

I met her at a Return to Happiness workshop, held in La Chinita, a *barrio* of Apartadó in northwest Colombia, that I was running with a handful of volunteers. The volunteers were all thirteen or fourteen years old. The kids were mostly under ten, and had been forced out of their homes in the surrounding villages by the violence. It was ironic that their families looked for safety in La Chinita, where some of the biggest massacres of the war had occurred.

Juanita was about seven years old, dark and plump, with tight black curls. She was a recent arrival in La Chinita and showed many signs of distress. When all the other kids were running around, playing games, singing songs, and painting pictures, Juanita sat on her own, sometimes watching the action, but mostly just staring at the dirt floor. Her face showed no expression, no feeling. She looked numb and disconnected.

The Return to Happiness project was set up by UNICEF and the Catholic Church in 1997 after violence in our region forced thousands of families to flee from their homes. The project trained hundreds of teenagers and adults as volunteer "play" therapists, who ran workshops for displaced children. Each workshop followed the same basic pattern. First there were games and songs, then painting, and then we played with toys. Usually we played in groups but with kids like Juanita, the really sad ones, we played one-on-one.

I sat on the floor beside her and showed her the *bolsillo*, the knapsack full of materials that every volunteer carries. "Look what I've got in here," I told her, but she didn't seem interested.

I took out the rag dolls, the puppets, and the wooden toys — the donkey cart, the helicopter, the truck, the motorbike, and the boat. I started to play with them. I sat the man on the donkey cart and pushed him along. I flew the helicopter. I put the rag mother with the rag children, and let them hug one another. Then I offered her the rag family.

She looked at them for a while, then she picked up the rag man and sat him on the donkey cart. She pushed him along, then burst into tears.

"Don't worry," I told her. "We can play again later."

She didn't answer but she sat quietly while I read aloud the story of "The Happy Monkey." This is about a monkey who wants to be brave and strong but the only way he knows how to do this is to be aggressive. None of the other animals like him but eventually, with the help of a wise macaw, he learns how to be a true friend, by trusting others.

While I told the story I used the puppets of the monkey and the wise macaw to illustrate their roles. I introduced the macaw puppet to Juanita as a special friend that she could tell secrets to. Some of the kids find it easier to talk to a puppet than they do to a real person.

That first time I don't think Juanita took in half of what I was saying, but the first lesson of doing this work is that you have to give the kids time. Afterwards, I always sat with Juanita when we held a workshop in La Chinita. At first she didn't talk at all. Then she began to mumble, speaking through the toys. She often broke down and couldn't go on.

Finally, after weeks of playing, I thought I understood the painful story of what had happened to her family.

The family was on the donkey cart: her father, her mother, Juanita, and her sister. A helicopter came and flew around them, making a loud whirring sound. When she flew the wooden helicopter, Juanita made the whirring sound through her teeth. Her whole face was screwed up with the effort.

The family was frightened by the noise and the way the helicopter circled overhead. Her father stopped the cart and they all ran away to hide in the banana fields. She was with her mother and sister. Her father was on the other side of the road.

The helicopter landed some way off. The men came and one of them found her father. Juanita and her mother and sister stayed hidden but they saw everything. She saw them drag her father out of the field. She bent the tiny rag arms of the rag doll behind his head, just the way her father's arms had been. The commander of the armed men came along and he pushed Juanita's father onto the ground, facedown. Then he took out a gun and shot him three times. Every time the rag man went "pow!" with his gun, his whole body jumped with the force of his weapon. The rest of the family watched helplessly from their hiding places.

After the armed men had gone, Juanita gathered the rag dolls that stood for herself, her sister, and her mother, and ran them to the father doll. They fell on him and cried and cried until their mother said they must go, must leave, must run away. They fled, abandoning everything, and traveled first by boat and then in the back of a truck, until they came to La Chinita.

There wasn't much I could do to help Juanita, aside from playing with her, paying attention to her, and encouraging her to join in with the other kids. I had been trained to keep notes on how she was playing, what she seemed to be saying, and how her mood was, and I gave this information to the project psychologist. But the psychologist was overwhelmed. So many children were affected by the war, and some were even more disturbed than Juanita. It was quite a long time before the psychologist got around to her. By that time, Juanita seemed to be improving, sometimes even joining in our games. Then one day she just disappeared with her family. Probably they went to another town or even to the city, but no one knew for sure. It happens a lot these days. People are here and then they leave and you never find out what happened to them.

There is a lot about this work that is very sad. Sometimes it is hard to measure any kind of improvement in the kids. It is hard to know if we are really achieving anything. I've sometimes thought about giving it all up because I need to spend more time on my studies. My family is also poor and so I need to earn money to buy supplies for school. But I also wonder what would happen to these children if I and other young people didn't do this work. Most psychologists and sociologists don't want to come to Apartadó to work, because they say it is too dangerous.

I was born in Montería, a large town about ninety miles east of Apartadó. My father had a small shop where he sold household goods and fixed motorbikes. We never had much money. My father often came home drunk, got into fights with my mother, cursed, and sometimes whipped me. When I was nine he left us and I never saw him much after that. A few years later he was murdered during a robbery. I was angry with him for abandoning us, but his death meant I lost him forever. I still miss him.

We had no money after my father left so my mother began selling our household goods and furniture to buy food. Then she started selling her clothes. One day she told me she had to leave for a while, so that we could make a new start somewhere else. She wanted me to stay in the house in Montería. My mother promised to send me money and to telephone every week, then she left. I was ten years old and for nearly a year I lived entirely alone.

I missed my mother desperately. I cried hard whenever I saw a photograph of her, or some of her clothes. I had to learn how to cook for myself, standing on a chair because I couldn't reach the stove. I washed my own clothes by hand and cleaned the house. I decided that if I was very good, took care of the house, and studied hard at school, my mother might come back. She called every week but she always asked me to wait a bit longer. I knew she had good reasons for being away, but I was miserable. I never told anyone I was alone, not even my friends or my teachers. I was afraid that if anyone knew then robbers would come and my mother would never return.

She left me in February 1995 and came back the following December. I couldn't believe it when she walked through the door. I held onto her, touching and hugging her. She had been thin when she went away but she came back quite plump. She told me that we were going to live on a banana plantation near Apartadó. She had a job selling meals to the workers and she was living with a man who would become my stepfather.

The tiny house that my mother took me to was unlike any other place I had ever lived. Montería was noisy and crowded. There were always people out on the streets, music blasting from bars, people selling anything and everything on the sidewalks. But the plantation was quiet and slow by day. Nothing ever happened there, and I wasn't used to the sounds of the countryside by night.

I'd heard that armed groups sometimes came to farms like that and abducted children who were then forced to become soldiers. I'd heard of massacres of farm workers and I suffered from recurring nightmares in which an armed group appeared on the farm, dragged us out of our house, and killed us all. It was also strange to be living so closely with my mother and this man. He wasn't bad to me but I felt like an intruder. I realized that even though I had missed my mother, I had almost become used to being alone.

After only a few weeks my mother explained to me that I would have to leave. It was for my own good, she said, because I needed to go to a decent school. She had arranged for me to live with a cousin in Apartadó and to enter the ninth grade at the José Celestino Mutis secondary school. I didn't complain. Apartadó wasn't as big as Montería but at least it was a town.

Looking back, I know that even though I suffered when I was left alone, it also forced me to grow up quickly. Now I was determined to do well, study hard, and get ahead.

Soon after entering the school I was elected to represent my class in the student government. A couple of months later, in April 1996, Graça Machel came to Apartadó.* That visit transformed a lot of our lives, because it put Apartadó on the map as a place where young people were really trying to do something to make peace. Many of us trained as promoters of the rights of children. We went into schools and taught other kids about their rights and why we should all vote in the Children's Mandate.

---

* See Farlis: The Line Between Now and Tomorrow

Really big changes began happening for me in 1997, when I was thirteen years old and the Return to Happiness program started. By that time, many displaced families were turning up in Apartadó, Turbo, and other towns in the region. Every day we would see them arrive on donkey carts, in trucks and buses, or on foot. There were old people, babies, young children, pregnant women. Many were wounded, emotionally if not physically, and stunned from what had happened to them. All they had left were the things they were carrying. They had been driven from their homes by the struggle between the armed groups who were competing for control of the land. These groups used the most vicious methods to force people to leave. They didn't care what happened to the children or what they saw: They would even kill the parents in front of the children and then leave the children with the bodies.

Most of the displaced moved in with relatives, rented small rooms, or constructed their own shelters. In a few places special camps were set up. The municipal sports center in Turbo, a town about twenty miles from Apartadó, was transformed into a massive dormitory for about four hundred people.

As Return to Happiness volunteers we were given training,

supplies, and T-shirts identifying us as part of the program. The demand for the workshops was huge. I recruited a dozen other volunteers from the Celestino School, helped in their training, and then organized the workshops that we ran in La Chinita and elsewhere. During 1997–1998 our group worked with more than a thousand children and we were always getting requests to do more.

Even if it was hard, working in the program gave us something constructive to do in a situation where we could otherwise feel quite helpless. Also, trying to understand the difficulties of these children helped me to understand my own problems. I had always found it hard to talk about what had happened to me when my mother left, and when my father was murdered, but listening to other kids helped me to open up.

By the time I began volunteering in the Return to Happiness program, I was living in a *barrio* known as Primero de Mayo (First of May) because that was the day on which squatters had invaded and seized the land. My mother and stepfather had been among them and together we had built a small wooden house.

Although I lived in Primero de Mayo, I had chosen to run the workshops in La Chinita because that was where many displaced children were living. But Apartadó was a deeply divided town. Different *barrios* were often associated with support for particular armed groups. People were sometimes suspicious of those who came from other *barrios*. It didn't make sense to some that we would do this work just to help children — any children.

After about a year of working in La Chinita I began to receive threats. People told me, "We hear it is getting risky for you over here." I got anonymous phone calls telling me that I wasn't welcome in La Chinita anymore, or that I should "look out for my health." When I left my house I felt as if I were being followed, although I never had any proof. I didn't know if the risk was real or not. Maybe it was just "talk," but I became so frightened I couldn't sleep at night or concentrate on my studies. Everything seemed suspicious. I spoke with the coordinator of the Return to Happiness program and it was decided that I should stop working in La Chinita. I concentrated instead on trying to improve conditions for children in my own *barrio* — I developed a proposal and raised the funds that allowed us to put up a playground. I also volunteered at the office of the Return to Happiness program and for a while, produced a newsletter about different activities of youth volunteers. Via fax and eventually the Internet, we were able to keep at least some young people in the region in touch with what was happening in the Children's Movement for Peace in other parts of the country.

The idea that teenagers should play an active role in peacemaking had been an important principle for us in Apartadó ever since the visit of Graça Machel, but adults interpret "participation" in different ways. Some adults were sympathetic and believed in us; they listened to our ideas and tried to work with us. Others thought that because we were "only children" we should do as we were told. They felt that our opinions counted for nothing.

When Gloria Cuartas was the mayor of Apartadó, she really wanted to work with young people. It was because of her that Farlis became the first Child Mayor of Apartadó in April 1996. At the same time, even though I was only twelve years old, I had become the Secretary General of the children's government of Apartadó. We thought that this children's government was an important breakthrough for young people in the town. Gloria Cuartas was always receptive to hearing about our ideas and experiences. But when she left office, and another mayor took over, we no longer had the same access. We had no rights under the law to have our opinions taken into account. It depended entirely on the personal views of the adults concerned.

We never had any more elections for the children's government in Apartadó (although these have been held successfully in other towns in Colombia). Farlis kept the title of Child Mayor until she turned eighteen, and then there was no more Child Mayor. I am now sixteen and still use my title of Secretary General sometimes, because it can help. I used it just a few weeks ago to help my school donate several blackboards to a very poor school in another *barrio*. Yet my title as Secretary General is really an empty one, because there is no other official left in the children's government except me.

I had been working in the peace movement for more than four years and frankly I had become quite depressed. My life had become so serious. I felt unable to have fun like other young people. If I wasn't studying, I was selling hot dogs to make money to buy school supplies, or working with children, or volunteering at the Return to Happiness office. I never went dancing. I never just hung out with other people my age, not unless it was to plan a peacemaking event. The work seemed endless.

Then, in September 2000, I was invited to go to the United Nations in New York to talk about my work. There were four of us representing the Children's Movement for Peace: Mayerly* came from Bogotá, Sebastian from Medellín, Leonardo from Mapiripan, and myself. We talked about our lives and our work in front of many United Nations delegates, and showed the film *Soldiers of Peace: A Children's Crusade* that CNN had made about our Movement in 1999.

Each of us had different experiences of violence, and very different ways of making peace. Leonardo, who is thirteen years old, talked about a terrible massacre in his village that forced everyone to leave. He went to Mapiripan with his family. There he got involved in a project that established "territories of peace" in public parks and playgrounds. These were areas where children could go to solve conflicts without violence.

Sebastian had been shot in the head "by mistake" during a

* See Mayerly: After Milton

gang attack on his father's taxi. He now worked with Beto* in Medellín, helping primary school children to understand their rights. I talked about the murder of my father, and told the story of Juanita using the dolls and wooden toys from the Return to Happiness project.

Many people praised our work and told us that we were brave. I never really felt brave, but experiencing how other people saw us helped me to understand that what we are doing is important. People were kind and generous to us and for a few days we lived like tourists. We went to the top of the World Trade Center, took a boat tour to the Statue of Liberty, and visited a huge amusement park. It was so different from everything I know in Apartadó — so beautiful and extraordinary, like an illusion, a dream.

Back in Apartadó life is very much the same as it was before. I hold onto those images of New York. I don't ever want to forget them — yet I also feel as if my mind has been cleared of doubt. Many people in other countries are interested in and care about our work. It is wonderful to feel their affection and support. I told the other volunteers in Apartadó that we

* See Beto: Falling in Love With Life

have friends all over the world, more than we could possibly imagine.

Last week, ten of us sat down and planned a children's march against kidnapping. More than three hundred children and teenagers took part. We stopped the traffic as we walked through Apartadó calling for the right to life to be respected, for children to be kept out of the war, for our right to live in peace and freedom.

It was a great day.

## LETTERS FROM THE JUNGLE

THE THEATER WAS MASSIVE AND IN THE DARKNESS IT SEEMED to grow even more cavernous. We were huddled in family groups, hugging each other. Some people were already crying. The colonel walked up on the stage and read out the names of the sixty-one police officers and cadets who had been kidnapped during the storming of Mitú. With every name, a photograph appeared on the screen and one family group in the vast hall sighed or cried out because it was their son or husband or father or brother or lover.

I sat in the darkness with my father and mother and heard the Colonel speak "Hernando's" name. My mother gasped, "There he is!" His face appeared on the screen, looking like me as always, with the same nose and the same mouth. But this time he was looking back at us from far away, from a place we couldn't reach.

Then the camera slowly panned by all the faces, and each captive said a few words. Someone shouted out, "My son! My son is alive! What do I do now? My son is out there in the jungle!"

When Hernando came on the screen, it was as if everyone else in the theater disappeared and he was there only for us.

"Hello Mom, Dad, everyone," he said. "I'm doing fine. You don't have to worry. I miss you all very much but I'll be released soon. You just get on with your lives and don't let your spirits get you down because I'm going to be just fine. . . ."

Hernando's kidnapping has changed everything. It holds all of us hostage. We cannot think about anything else. I don't have conversations with my mother anymore because I know, before I begin, what she is thinking. The kidnapping colors all my dreams. When I eat I think, "What is he eating?" When I sleep I think, "How is he sleeping?"

Nothing can be right in our world until he comes back.

Hernando left school in 1994 and decided to join the police. He signed on to drive a patrol car. He never imagined he would be in combat. After his initial training he was supposed to join the highway police in Cartagena in the north. Then the commander called the new recruits to a meeting and asked which of them did not want to go to Cartagena. Now Cartagena is a beautiful coastal town, and one of Colombia's most popular tourist locations, but it is a long way from Bogotá. Hernando raised his hand, thinking that he would be posted closer to the capital. Instead he was told that he must go right away to Mitú. He had never even heard of the place.

Mitú is small garrison town, deep in the Amazon region, only thirty miles from the border with Brazil. For hundreds of miles in all directions there is nothing but rivers and the jungle. And Mitú is well inside territory that has been contested by the armed groups for more than forty years.

We were all afraid when Hernando was sent there, but for the first couple of years it turned out to be a peaceful place. Hernando made many friends and found a girlfriend. She worked at the hospital and also came from Bogotá. We have photographs of his life there. In one he is wearing swimming shorts and standing on the bank of the River Vaupés. Another shows him relaxed and happy with his fellow officers inside the police station.

Several journalists had been writing that Mitú had been

threatened — and given its location, I suppose it was inevitable that eventually the war would reach there — but none of us thought about it at the time. Hernando never gave the impression that there was any trouble. Even though he was so far away we spoke on the phone two or three times a week. In 1997 he came home on leave and stayed for a couple of months. He was due to come again on November 1, 1998, but that was the day that the town was attacked.

My mother was woken up that Sunday at dawn by a telephone call from my godfather. "Listen to the radio," he told her. "A battle is going on in Mitú."

My father was away but my mother woke me up and we spent the whole day in the house, listening to the radio and waiting for news. My older sister came over and made calls to the Red Cross and other places, trying to get information. At one point my mother announced she had had enough. She was going to get on a plane and fly out there to see what was happening.

"You can't go, mama," my sister told her. "They are still fighting. It's a war zone."

So my mother went back to waiting. The tears rolled

down her face. You could see she would not have minded walking right into the battle to pick up her son and bring him home.

She was thinking, "You can have your war, but let me have my child."

Instead we waited and learned that, during the attack on the police station, all the officers on duty had been killed. We didn't know if Hernando had been on duty or not; we didn't know if he was alive or dead. The town was virtually destroyed. People fled in droves. Still, the news only came through in bits and pieces. Two weeks passed before we knew Hernando had been kidnapped, that in the midst of the fighting he had been loaded into the back of a truck, apparently asleep or unconscious, and covered with ash from the explosions.

Until we knew for sure that he was safe, I was out of my mind with grief. I wept constantly. At times I was sure he was dead, then just as convinced that he must be alive. I was sure he would have been terrified in combat. He didn't belong in the war. I think he hardly understood it. I don't think any of us understand it.

I stayed away from school for a few weeks but when I went back I didn't tell anyone what had happened, not my teachers or my friends. I thought they wouldn't understand or care. My teachers only found out weeks later when my mother went to a PTA meeting and told them. Afterwards they were more supportive and sometimes asked if there was news, but I felt as if a gulf had opened up between me and other people who had not been touched directly by the war. I thought they could not possibly imagine what it was like to walk in my shoes.

I was involved in the peace movement long before Hernando was kidnapped. In 1995, when I was ten years old, I joined the Colombian Red Cross as a volunteer and started learning about international human rights — the rights people have to protection during war, the rights of children, and so on. I also became involved in the Free Air program. I learned about the environment, about damage to the ozone layer, recycling, and the problems of deforestation. I became a "multiplier," which means I organized seminars at my own and at other schools to pass on this information. Through the Colombian Red Cross I received training in how to work with other young people in an entertaining way, using colorful brochures and games that were fun as well as educational.

I became much more involved in peace activities in 1997, when I was about twelve years old. This was the year that the Citizen's Mandate was held and peace was suddenly on everyone's lips. At the Red Cross, a group of young volunteers were interviewed about our ideas towards peace. Their questions inspired me.

I decided that peace was really a state of mind. Peace depended on the way you saw things, and on how you responded to other people. If this was so, then it seemed to me that if should be possible for children and young people to do quite a lot to make peace, even without the help of adults.

In the Children's Mandate of 1996, nearly three million children and adolescents had voted for their rights and for peace. The Mandate was important, but it was only the first step. If we really wanted to make peace, I thought, we would need to change the way we felt inside.

I was very excited by this idea. I thought, "I can have big goals even though I am a kid."

I set up my peace project without the help of any other organization or adults, although the Red Cross was always helpful. To get permission to run peace seminars at my school I had to write letters to the rector and create a plan of action showing what I wanted to do, when I wanted to do it, and what the activities would be. Some teachers were doubtful whether other students would be interested, but plenty were. Mostly they were interested in themes like peaceful coexistence within the school and how we could get more unity. But I also used these sessions to promote the idea that peace is not just a word, it is something that we can all do.

I tried to keep the meetings dynamic. I knew from my other work with the Red Cross that I would get nowhere if I gave boring lectures. Gradually I began branching out into other schools and even organized some big meetings where large numbers of students got together to share ideas.

Sometimes I was able to help individual students. One girl called "Ana Dolores" had a lot of problems at home, where she was very badly abused. As a result, she was aggressive and destructive at school and was badly treated there as well. Her classmates often humiliated her.

I invited Ana Dolores to come to a forum that I was running during recess in the school theater. After that she began to trust and confide in me. That was how I learned about the abuse. She had never told anyone before.

Soon afterwards I arranged to give a talk to her class. I didn't identify Ana Dolores by name, but in a roundabout way I inferred that I was talking about her. I described some of the problems of living in a violent home and how this could make a person behave in a certain way at school. I said we could all help that person by understanding and listening to them. After that things changed. Her classmates became much more supportive and Ana Dolores became happier, at least at school.

After Hernando's kidnapping the peace project became much more important to me. I think the other students also took me more seriously because they knew I was affected by violence. It made them more interested. But I lost most of my friends because I stopped joking around in class. I also stopped going out unless it was to a peace meeting, or to volunteer for the Red Cross. I've mostly worked alone on the peace project, but recently more students have been asking what they can do to get involved.

# # #

I dream only good dreams about Hernando — that I walk into the house and he is by my side.

I lie on my bed, stare at the ceiling, and try to imagine where he is now, what he is doing.

I think about our lives growing up. I am sometimes even nostalgic for the fights we had, over who would get into the bathroom first, or over the way he used to pull the blankets off me when I was sleeping.

Sometimes I see someone who looks like him in the street and my heart jumps.

I wonder what it will be like for him when he comes back, how will he cope after being in the jungle for two years or more, without even seeing a bus?

I feel good about the peace work because I'll be able to show Hernando that I didn't sit around with my arms crossed while he was in captivity.


Three months after the kidnapping we heard that police head-quarters had received a videotape and letters from the victims of the Mitú kidnapping. At the time we thought that perhaps Hernando would be released soon. Many times since then negotiations have been held with the armed group holding him, yet years have passed and he is still not free. My mother got involved with *Asofamilas*, a support organization for families of the Mitú kidnap victims, and has participated in some negotiations herself. At least we have been able to send books, photos, and letters to him, and receive letters back.

So many people have been kidnapped in Colombia that a special radio station has been set up so that people can send messages to their loved ones in captivity. We have been on *Radio Recuerdo* (Radio Remember) and sent messages to Hernando. We know he has heard us.

In one letter he wrote, "It's wonderful to hear your voices [on the radio] and know that everybody is fine. Every night I wait for the program to start and listen to see if someone says hi to me. . . ."

He told us about his life. "Every day they wake us up at 6 A.M. to have breakfast and then you're left 'deprogrammed' because there's nothing to do apart from lie in a hammock thinking. . . . I play dominos but I get tired of playing them all the time even though there are some friends here who play like crazy all day long."

I have sent poems to him, to inspire him to stay confident and hopeful. I tell him that I listen to his advice and study hard. I was very glad when he recently wrote back and said, "I am happy you're doing so well at school. . . . That's where I went wrong. I regret not having made the most of my studies. . . . I really didn't like reading, for example . . . [yet] here I have read over thirty books of all different kinds and there are still more to read. I even get the dictionary and look up weird words that I don't know. . . . I would never have done this of my own accord before. . . ."

Even though he seems safe, I still worry. You never know what will happen. If I could talk to the people who are holding my brother I would ask them to have compassion and to understand the suffering they have caused.

I think that forgiveness is fundamental if we are to achieve peace. The war cannot come to an end without forgiveness. It is especially important for people like us who have suffered to forgive.

I think that this is what I am working for — I work for forgiveness.

## A WAY OF BEING FREE

WE LIVED AT THE FOOT OF A MOUNTAIN IN BOYACÁ, IN A small wooden house with three rooms: one for my parents, one for the five children, and the third for the farm tools. From the doorway I could see my grandfather's house, and another small dwelling half way up the mountain. There were fields of corn, yucca, blackberries, potatoes, and sugar cane, as well as many animals — hens, rabbits, cows, a horse, and the dog that followed my father everywhere.

We lived off the land and took water from the river running behind the house. My father earned some money selling wood to a man who took it to Bogotá in his truck. I used to watch my father heading down the valley towards the road — the horse loaded with wood walking in front of him, and the dog trailing behind. The horse had made that journey so often he knew the route by heart.

I went to school in a tiny hamlet called "Freedom," an

hour's walk from our farm. It was a one-room, one-teacher country school for kids in kindergarten through fifth grade. My cousin Jimmy was my best friend and at recess we took off across the field next to the school, running as fast as we could, screaming and yelling all the way. When the bell rang we dawdled back to class, or sometimes we didn't go at all. We climbed a tree at the edge of the field and stayed hidden — watching the other kids line up to go back inside. Then we had fun: climbing trees, eating oranges, and sometimes going down to the river to fish. The fishing was easy. We scooped them up in a sieve and slipped them into a jar.

We got punished for skipping class but we didn't care. It was always worth it.

My dad kept a piece of rope hanging from a nail in his room and used it to beat us kids for anything and everything. If I knew a beating was coming — because I hadn't cut grass for the horse or hadn't fed the chickens or just because my dad was in a bad mood — I ran off and hid in the cane field. While my dad stomped around the yard, yelling his head off, I took out my machete, hacked off a piece of sugar cane and lay there peacefully chewing out all the sweet juice. I still got the beating, but the edge of his anger would be gone and he didn't hit so hard.

I thought my life would never change, but one night when I was seven years old an army of men surrounded our house. They were tall and muscular, carrying guns; they had machetes hanging from their belts. There were dozens of them, maybe even a hundred. One of the biggest of them, wearing thick heavy boots and toting a massive gun, pushed open the door of our house and came inside.

He looked at us and at our house and then he said, "You've got to go. Get out of here by tomorrow. I'm coming back. Don't be here." He didn't shout or push us around. He didn't have to. We couldn't argue with him.

My parents and older brothers and sisters started packing up, grabbing whatever they could, trying to figure out what to take and what to leave. I didn't understand but everyone was in too much of a rush to explain.

Then I saw the rope. It was still hanging from its nail in my parents' room. My dad wasn't taking it!

"Hey!" I hissed at my brothers and sisters, "Hey look!

He's not taking the rope! He won't be able to beat us any-more!"

Man, I was so excited. I thought that maybe these men who were kicking us out of our home were doing me a big favor! Later, of course, I realized he didn't need that old piece of rope. He could hit us with anything, like his belt, which he did quite often. That was when I began to understand what we had lost by leaving Boyacá.

We took a bus to Bogotá the next day and at first we moved into my uncle's tiny apartment in the south of the city. It felt like a jail. The windows were small and murky. There wasn't anything to look at anyway, only the street and more buildings. The city lay out there and I wanted to rush out and explore. On the farm I could take off for a whole day, roaming the fields, climbing trees, playing in the rivers. I thought the city was the same. I wanted to get out there and learn the roads like I knew the trails back home. I would see where all those people were going. I would find the heart of it and really get to know it. But my mom and dad wouldn't let me go any further than the street corner. Most of the time they wouldn't even let me do that.

"No, you've been to the corner already. There's nothing to see. Sit down and shut up."

They made me stay inside the apartment. There was nothing to do. I was going crazy.

My uncle found us some rooms nearby and I started going to school. The kids teased me because of my accent. They called me "Boyaco" which is a really insulting way of describing someone from Boyacá. I tried to change the way I spoke so that I would fit in, but it was hard. In Boyacá I'd always had a lot of friends, but in Bogotá I didn't have any. I didn't care much. I figured I didn't need anyone. I ran my own life.

My dad got a job as a security guard and my parents used the money from the sale of our farm — about six hundred dollars — to buy a plot where we started building a small house. The first time my mother took me there, my heart jumped. Around the corner from the house was an open abandoned space, almost a field. There were even a few tethered goats grazing in the middle. One day, I slipped out of the house and ran to that "field." I stood on one corner, staring across at the other side, maybe two hundred yards away. Then I ran, as fast as I could, jumping over the rough littered ground, over the nettles and weeds, through the mud, yelling my head off. All the way I was thinking of Jimmy and that field next to my school in Boyacá. For a moment I had a taste of that same freedom, but then it was gone.

Our *barrio* was called Patio Bonito, which means "Pretty Terrace," but there wasn't much that was pretty about the place or our lives. It must have been tough on my dad to be kicked off the farm like that, but I didn't understand it at the time. I just saw him coming home drunk and taking his disappointment and anger out on all of us. I learned to depend on him less, but I wanted to help my mother.

When I was ten years old I started working. I thought everyone in the family should help out. Besides, life was easier if you had some coins in your pocket. One girl at school worked for a businessman who gave her peas to sell and they split the profits. I did the same. I took as many packets of peas as I could carry and walked the streets from Corabastos market towards the Candelaria Nueva. When all the peas were gone, I caught the bus back.

It was hard work and not always safe. Sometimes I got robbed and lost everything, so when I was twelve I started working inside Corabastos market as a street seller — I'd heard it was more profitable. I didn't understand then about the way things worked in the market. I didn't know there was a war going on in there.

Corabastos is the biggest market in Colombia, maybe in the whole of Latin America. Thousands of people work there. Millions of dollars (billions of pesos) change hands there every week. Most business is done by the big merchants who operate huge warehouses. Smaller merchants run vegetable and fruit shops in the streets clustered around the warehouses. Then there are people like me who try to sell a few bags of vegetables here and there on the street.

Most mornings I got to the market by four o'clock, when the sky was still pitch-dark but the lights at the market would be blazing, with the trucks rolling in and out, produce getting loaded and unloaded, the streets jammed with vans and carts and the air tasting of diesel, vegetables, and the cold mist of the morning.

Everywhere there would be kids working. Kids hauling sacks of beans and potatoes. Kids laying out the produce on the stalls. Kids breaking into food fights and sometimes the adults joining in. Rotten fruit of any kind flew through the air, but tomatoes had the best effect, especially when they splattered on the back of someone's neck. Mostly it was fun but sometimes a food fight broke into a real fight and someone's blood would be on the ground.

Every day I saw violence. My second day in the market, a mob fell on an eighteen-year-old boy who had some marijuana, and they beat him to a pulp. Another time they caught a thief and cut him with machetes until he was almost dead, but not quite. Another thief was badly beaten, then almost drowned in the tank where they wash the potatoes. Then he was forced to walk up and down the streets of Corabastos shouting "I am a thief! I am a thief!"

The small merchants hated the street sellers because we undercut their prices. They paid the security guards, the "vultures," to push us around, to steal our vegetables, and to take our money. It happened all the time. Once they took three hundred packs of peas from my mother and me.

I never thought much about peace but I didn't like the injustice I saw in the market. I didn't like the wariness I had to have because I never knew where the violence would be coming from. I didn't like it when a mob ganged up on a person and beat them almost to death. No matter what that person had done, it didn't seem right. In a way it was just like the armed group that ganged up against my family and forced us off our land. We were weak. We couldn't do anything to protect ourselves. There was no justice back there in Boyacá and no justice inside Corabastos either. The strongest and the richest always won. The poorest and the weakest always lost. Most of the time the street sellers were at the bottom of the heap and the kids who were street sellers were the most vulnerable of all.

I didn't have much time for thinking about these things or anything else except working, going to school, and sleeping (sometimes even in school!). But in 1997, when I was twelve, I started going to a Saturday workshop for working children. I went because some friends of my mother's said it would be good for me. I didn't mind listening to their advice but I had no expectations.

The workshop was free and held at the Corabastos school, located inside the market. On the first day María Eugenia, who ran the project, gave me a money belt so I could keep my cash safe. That impressed me. There were three teachers: one taught music — how to play the harmonica, flute, guitar, or xylophone, another taught puppet-making, and the other showed us how to draw on disposable plates. I liked it. It was a change from all the other pressures in my life. In the beginning there were only a few of us kids at the workshop, but soon there were more than fifty.

After six months, María Eugenia asked me if I wanted to represent the working children of Corabastos on a special council of young people who were part of the Children's Movement for Peace. The organization she worked with and which supported our workshops — Defense of Children International — had been invited to send a youth delegate to the council. They had chosen me.

I hadn't been chosen by anyone for anything before but it was okay with me. Through the Council I met Farlis, Juan Elias, Mayerly, Johemir, Wilfrido, and a lot of other young people involved in peace activities: Iván Darío and Gloria from the Scouts, José Luis from the Red Cross, Monica and Marta from World Vision, Deivy from Profamilia, Dilia from Redepaz, Javier and Camilo from the Colegio San Bartolomé,

Nicolas from the Lincoln School, and up to thirty others, between ages twelve and seventeen.

The Council met about once a month, usually in the UNICEF office in northern Bogotá. We learned from one another about different ways of making peace. Deivy was a peer counselor who helped other adolescents learn about their health and positive relationships. He said that this was peacemaking because it helped to reduce relationship-violence between boyfriends and girlfriends, as well as teenage pregnancy, a major cause of violence in the home.

Iván Darío had written a project proposal, gotten the funding, and set up an arts center in his *barrio*. He thought of this as peacemaking because when people were involved in creative arts they felt better about themselves and were less interested in violence. I guess that idea matched what was happening with the working children in Corabastos. Some of the parents had even told María Eugenia that the behavior of their children had improved since they started coming to the Saturday workshop.

Gloria visited schools and told stories about the war that she had made up herself, because she thought this would help kids in Bogotá become more aware of the damage the war was doing. Monica and Marta were "peace constructors" who helped children in their *barrios* learn how to resolve conflicts without violence. Dilia ran a radio show at her school and had taken part in workshops and conferences all over the place, speaking out about the rights of children.

In the beginning, it wasn't easy to describe how I was trying to help peace. For me it was more like a daily struggle to stay out of trouble, sell some peas, and get to school. But I took what I was learning at the Council back to Corabastos. María Eugenia fixed me up with a microphone and I talked to all the other kids at the Saturday workshop about how a lot of our rights were being abused, especially our right not to have to work when we were under the legal age. But we were only working because our families were poor. We had no choice — I would not have been able to go to school if I didn't work — so this really meant that the poverty of our families was also an abuse of our rights.

I don't think any of us voted in the Children's Mandate, because we didn't know about it or didn't understand it. After I explained the idea, it was clear that the right to peace would be the most popular in our group. If we could take the violence out of our lives we would all be a lot better off.

Some mornings the "vultures" fell on the street sellers in massive groups. They ran down the street in a terrifying gang, stealing from us and shoving us about. Not long ago a five-year-old girl was killed when the vultures were on the rampage. The street sellers assumed the vultures had killed her and went on the attack, armed with bottles and rocks. The smaller merchants came in on the side of the vultures, the big merchants sided with the street sellers, and a miniature "war of Corabastos" broke out. The police came and at first seemed to be on the side of the vultures, but then they switched over to the street sellers and the big merchants. They beat the vultures with their clubs and fired tear gas pellets.

In the middle of the battle I came out of Corabastos school with María Eugenia. We saw some of the vultures running away and bleeding. That day the street sellers scored a victory, but we didn't win the battle. The vultures returned and it was as bad as ever.

I decided to move out of the market to get away from the

violence. I still go to Corabastos early every morning and buy half a sack of peas from a wholesaler, but I take it to the Plaza de Flores to sell. It is much calmer there, much better for business, and I have made some good friends among the other pea sellers. All of them are older than me but we fool around and have a good time. I work until eleven. Then I go home, change my clothes, and go to school for the afternoon. On a good day, I make around five dollars. I give two-thirds to my mother and keep a third for myself. Since I was twelve years old I have paid for all my own clothes and supplies for school.

In 1997, José Ramos Horta came to Colombia. He is from East Timor, a small island in the Pacific Ocean. For years he had been living in exile, working peacefully for the freedom of his people.* In 1996 he was awarded the Nobel Peace Prize for this work. The following year, while visiting Colombia, José met many members of the Children's Movement for Peace. We told him about the Children's Mandate, how nearly three million children had voted for their rights and how this had inspired many adults to work for the Citizen's Mandate.

* East Timor was invaded by Indonesian troops in 1975 and was ruled by Indonesia until 1999.

We explained the different ways in which young people were trying to make peace in different parts of the country. José Ramos Horta told us that he had not realized until he came to Colombia that children could be such a powerful force for peace. In January 1998, he wrote to the Nobel Committee in Oslo, nominating the Children's Movement for Peace for the Nobel Peace Prize. We think that this was the first time that children had been nominated for such an award, and José has nominated the Movement for the award every year, ever since.

Then, in February 2000, I went with four other representatives of the Children's Movement for Peace to receive an award from the queen of Spain. Since the Movement began in 1996 quite a lot of us have been overseas but when I heard that I'd been chosen to go to Spain, I thought it was a joke so I didn't tell anyone. What could I say anyway? For instance, to the men who work beside me in the Plaza de Flores,

"I'm going to miss a few days next week because I have to go over to Spain to pick up a prize from the queen." They would think I was crazy!

As the day got nearer it began to sink in. As usual I hauled my peas to the plaza, and asked the passers by, "Do you want to buy some peas?" but inside I was thinking, "Next week I'll be in Madrid talking to the queen!"

We had a lot of fun on that trip and Queen Sofia was very friendly as she presented the Children's Movement for Peace with a medal called the Grand Order for Social Solidarity. This was a prize awarded by the Spanish government to organizations that have improved conditions in their countries. Afterwards we had a press conference but I was overwhelmed and became completely tongue-tied. If I had the chance now I would explain to those journalists that I understand my limitations. Of course it is hard for children to make peace! I know I can't end the conflict in Corabastos, but I can help other working children by assisting María Eugenia at the Saturday workshop. I can persuade other kids not to become part of a group that imposes violence and injustice on others who are poor and weak. I can let other children and teenagers know that they can become a part of the movement just by doing something to help others in their communities. I would explain that of course it is great to receive prizes, but for every child in Colombia the ultimate prize is peace itself.

A couple of times I went back to my grandfather's place in Boyacá for a holiday but the last time I went, about three years ago, all that was left of our house were a few sticks and some poles. The man we sold the farm to neglected the crops. Everything was disorganized and overgrown. If you don't look after these things they fall apart.

I used to think of getting a small farm myself one day but I've got used to the city now. I dream of going to other places, and of learning new things. Sometimes I dream about becoming an astronaut and traveling to Jupiter, or else about becoming a magician.

I don't know any tricks yet but that magician, David Copperfield, came to Bogotá recently. He knows how to make people disappear. I thought, "If I could learn that trick, then maybe I could learn how to make the war disappear."

## SAVED FROM DROWNING

PEOPLE WHO BELONG TO ONE OF THE ARMED GROUPS gather not far from my house. I hear their vehicles and right away I get off the street, get inside my house, shut the door, watch television, or even go to bed. I don't want them to see me or talk to me or ask me anything. If I run into one of those armed groups I could fall into a trap. They could ask me why don't I join them and it would be hard for me to find an answer they would accept.

The only guys around here who have managed to stay out of the conflict are those who have stayed off the streets. If we have girlfriends, we go to their houses to visit, and then we go straight home. We always get home early. It is the only way to stay out of the war.

When I was about nine years old I thought about joining one of the armed groups because I heard that they paid good money. Some of my friends joined. They got hold of false papers that said they were fourteen years old, when really they were only nine or ten. They were annoyed with me for not going with them because I was always big for my age, my family is very poor, and I'm black. They thought I would be an excellent recruit. But by the time I was nine years old I was already working weekend shifts on a construction site. Edwin was my boss and he was like a father to me. He advised me against joining up and I was glad I listened. Of the eight children I knew who signed on, six are dead.

It is terrible but natural for guys around here to think of the war as a job option. We have grown up surrounded by violence. A few years ago *sicarios* (assassins) began riding into our *barrio* on their motorbikes and shooting people just because they were on the street. Armed groups killed people they suspected of supporting their enemies. They killed parents in front of their children. They killed the children too and even newborn babies. Girls as young as eleven or twelve were getting pregnant because of their relationships with men in the armed groups. Most of them got involved, like the boys, just because they were out on the street. They couldn't say no to sex. If they refused, they paid with their blood.

Some of them were tortured and killed anyway for having relationships with men on the "wrong" side.

No matter how hard young people tried to stay out of the conflict, sometimes it was impossible to avoid. One day I was walking to school when a truck pulled up in front of me. One of the men lifted a weapon. He was turning it towards me, but then another man said, "No, not him, he isn't the one . . ." and they drove away. I was almost killed by mistake.

Two years ago on Good Friday there was a battle in our *barrio* and two of my friends were killed in the crossfire: Javier was fourteen years old and Mauricio was seventeen. Every day, innocent young people like Javier and Mauricio are getting caught and killed in the war. Every day, guys my age are deciding to join, or are being forced to join, and so the war goes on.

My family lived in a tiny house in Apartadó in northwest Colombia. We were always poor. My dad and mom were always fighting. Finally, when I was seven years old, my dad left us. At least we had peace at home but we were poorer than ever.

I started working every morning, from four A.M. to six

A.M., banging on doors in the *barrio* and trying to sell the deep-fried snacks that we call *buñuelos*. It was lousy work. I was lucky if I made fifty cents a day, and I was always exhausted at school. I failed a lot of classes. I was angry about my dad, about our poverty. I was exhausted by work and did a lot of things that year that made me feel ashamed.

There was a girl in my grade, a couple of years older than me. I liked her but she didn't like me. The truth was that she didn't like black people, so I used to trouble her. I'd give her hair a pull when I was passing. Once when I did this she grabbed hold of my hand and sank her teeth into me. It hurt so much, I yelled out loud and on a reflex I punched her, right in the face.

It was horrible. I'd never hit a girl before and I never meant to hit her. I didn't know what to do or say. Her face was really messed up. About a week later I saw her in the street with her parents. They were looking hard at me, with a lot of hatred and disgust. I felt so ashamed. I don't know how I had the nerve but I walked right up to them and I apologized, to the girl and to her parents, and asked for their forgiveness. I don't think they forgave me, but I felt better anyway.

In those days I only went to school to play or to fight. I

never bothered about learning but this began to change after Edwin gave me a break. Edwin was a huge guy, originally from Cartagena. He lived across the street from us and ran a small construction company. Even though I was only seven years old I was always asking him for a job.

"Nah," he told me, "You're too young. You should be studying. You can't do this work."

One weekend I stowed away in his truck and he didn't find out until we got to the work site. He was angry because he didn't want to waste his time taking me back home.

"Don't take me then," I told him. "Let me stay." I've always been a joker. I like to laugh and have fun, and even though Edwin was mad I could still make him laugh. In the end, he let me stay.

"Get a broom and sweep that trash," he told me. So I swept the trash and did everything I could to be helpful. Eventually he agreed to hire me on weekends and holidays as well.

Edwin cared about how I was doing at school. He asked about my grades, encouraged me, and gave me good advice. It was because of Edwin that I became more responsible. I always had fun but I stopped fooling around in a destructive way. The teachers learned they could trust me and sometimes left me in charge of the class while they went out on errands. I liked it. I started thinking that maybe one day I would become a teacher or a social worker.

Edwin told me that I shouldn't do heavy work on the construction site but that was one piece of advice I wouldn't take. I wanted to be one of the men. I wanted to prove I was as strong as they were. If they could carry heavy sacks of cement, then I could too. But Edwin was right. I was too young to do such heavy work and I injured my back. In 1994, when I was eleven, it got so bad that for two months I couldn't walk at all. I went to the hospital in Montería for treatment and slowly recovered. I learned how to walk and run again, but it isn't the same as before.

Since my back is permanently damaged, I won't have to go in the army, but the other armed groups don't give exemptions.

In 1996, when I was thirteen years old, there was a lot of activity in Apartadó schools because of the visit of Graça Machel.* I went to one of the meetings. They gave out T-shirts and talked to us about child rights but it didn't excite me. I told my friends that I wasn't going to get involved. I felt

* See Farlis: The Line Between Now and Tomorrow

differently a year later when hundreds of displaced families came pouring into Apartadó. I went along to a huge meeting of more than two thousand young people held in the sports arena in Apartadó. Nidya Quiroz was there, a short, pale Ecuadorean woman who worked with UNICEF. She talked about training young people in play therapy so that we could help children affected by the war. They wanted volunteers who would dance, sing, and play games, to help the children cope with trauma.

This was much more interesting to me. I couldn't give a lecture on child rights but I knew how to entertain kids. I like kids. I like their energy and sense of fun, and I thought that maybe I could get a child to open up to me.

I went through the training course for the Return to Happiness program* and began working with displaced children in my *barrio*. At first there was a lot of fear. We wore T-shirts identifying us as Return to Happiness volunteers, but children and parents in our *barrio* thought we were officials. So we dressed up in costumes instead and acted out in a funny way what was happening in the *barrio*. It drew the kids out, made them laugh, and helped us to win their trust.

---

* See Johemir: Journeys Far From Home

As the workshops became more popular, I recruited more youth volunteers. Within a couple of years I was supervising nearly eighty of them, and together we were working with up to four thousand children.

The workshop we ran last week in Rio Grande was typical. Rio Grande is a small community just outside Apartadó. A teacher at the primary school there had asked us to come because they had recently received a lot of displaced children. I took fifteen volunteers. More would have come but they didn't have the fifty cents needed for the bus fare.

About forty kids were waiting for us. Since this was their first session they had no idea what to expect. We walked into the room with a lot of joy and energy. We were shouting and laughing, and right away the kids caught our mood.

"Okay!" we shouted, "Okay, we are going to PLAY! Who wants to PLAY?!!!"

"We do!" they screamed.

"What?" I said, "I can't hear you! Was that a mouse talking? Was that an ant? I said, Do you want to PLAY?"

And they yelled, "YES!!!"

Then I calmed them down with a prayer. I asked God to

protect us, to help us to do our best, to protect the children who were getting hit by their parents, to ask the mothers and fathers not to hit the children again but to explain themselves instead, and for everyone to behave themselves in the workshop and to fully participate.

We all said the "amen" and moved straight into a traditional singing game: *La Pulga* (The Flea). I danced into the middle of the circle of kids and volunteers, singing, "I've got a flea and it's biting me here!"

"*¡Hueso!*" they all yelled, which means "Bone!" because of the rattling of your bones as you itch around with the flea bite.

"And it's biting me there!"

"*¡Hueso!*"

I went into contortions showing all the places where the flea was biting. Every move made the kids laugh. Then I picked one of them, and yelled, "Now the flea is jumping onto you!"

"*¡HUESO!*" they screamed as the chosen child moved into the middle of the ring, singing and dancing to show where that flea was biting.

After a few games like *La Pulga*, the kids settled down and

we moved on to painting. We let them paint with anything —
with leaves, twigs, brushes, and fingers. They painted anything they wanted, on their own or in groups.

One child painted a black heart. I asked him what it was
and he said, "That is my heart because I am evil." He felt that
way because of the violence in his home. He thought it was
his fault.

Another boy who was about eight years old had seen his
father tortured, murdered, cut in pieces with a machete, the
parts put into a flour sack, and tossed into the river. He drew a
picture that showed what had happened. Another picture
showed a boy who was asleep at home when men came into
the house and killed his dad.

I've met a lot of troubled children through this work but
"Jacinta" is special for me. She had been born with much
darker skin than her parents and, because of this, they had
abandoned her. She lived with her grandmother, who had
never allowed the child to forget what her parents had done. I
heard her story for the first time when she told it to the macaw
puppet during one of the workshops. She said to him, "It upsets

me because I see the other children being taken to school by their parents, but I never have my mother or father to take me."

She said she would never forgive them. "They are my parents and should not have done this to me." She was right, but she was in so much pain it was harming her. She was doing badly at school and often got into fights. Once she even hit me.

I told her that I knew what it felt like to be rejected. I told her what it was like for me when my father left us. I said, "It makes you hate everyone but you end up hurting yourself even more."

I see Jacinta regularly but life is very hard for her. She has to cope with too much for such a young child — the violence of our community, the abandonment by her parents, poverty, and racism. Racism is all over Colombia. If the war ends, this country will still face a huge struggle against discrimination.

Jacinta and other children who are deeply troubled are referred to the project psychologist, but they also continue coming to our workshops. With patience and lots of attention, we do our best to get them involved in the activities. We believe that, if they can learn to play like children again, they can begin that return to happiness.

The work is sometimes so hard that I think I can't take anymore. We volunteers have our own workshops to help us cope and relax and let go of our emotions. Many of us cry, loudly and openly and with one another. We let loose all the anger we feel. Many say that they are angry with God for the way He has allowed so many young children to suffer. They say that God is unfair. But it isn't God who is hurting these children. Other people are doing it. Sometimes their own parents are doing it.

In January 1999, a massive earthquake hit the coffee belt region of Colombia. A thousand people were killed and tens of thousands lost their homes. I was one of thirty volunteers from the Return to Happiness program who went to Pereira to help children who had been traumatized by the earthquake. We worked alongside local teenagers, most of them Red Cross volunteers, so that they would be able to carry on the work after we had gone. Using the rag dolls, bricks, and stones, the children showed us how the buildings had fallen down on top of them, how their relatives had been buried, how they had lost their friends and everything they owned. Many of them were terrified of stepping into any building other than a tent. They talked about the day the earth cracked open and the world seemed to end.

One day, a boy in my group got very angry with a girl who was showing how the earthquake had destroyed her house.

"You think that is something?" he yelled at her. "That's nothing. It's nothing!" Then he ran away.

I spoke to some of the Red Cross volunteers, and found out where the boy lived. After the session was over, I went looking for him. "David" was eleven years old and living in a temporary shelter with his mother, brother, and sister. At first he didn't want to see me or talk to me, but I sat down with him and gradually learned what had happened. His father had been murdered in front of the family by one of the armed groups, and they had been forced to abandon their small farm. David wanted to avenge his father. "I will wait until I am sixteen and then I will find them and kill them all."

"But if you kill someone," I told him, "then their people will come after you and might kill the rest of your family too. Killing only leads to more killing."

"I can't let them live," he replied. "I have to kill them no matter what."

He wasn't going to be talked out of killing so I took another route. I played games with him. I played *La Pulga* and all the other singing games. They made him laugh so hard. He really began to enjoy himself. I began to see that when he was serious and thinking about his father he was like someone who was drowning. It was only when he was playing the games and having fun like a child that he was really himself.

I was in Pereira for just over three weeks and spent almost all my free time with David. When it was time for me to leave I found it hard to say goodbye. I didn't even see him on my last day, but he sent me a letter. He wrote that our friendship meant a lot to him and that he had realized that it would not solve anything if he killed his father's killers.

It is second nature to be careful when you live in a community like mine. When we hold meetings for the volunteers, for instance, we make sure people know that we are not re-cruiting for one of the armed groups. During those meetings we have a lot of fun. We write and sing love songs. We stage clown shows and do everything to show we are interested in peace, not in war.

Soon after I returned from Pereira, I decided I wanted to do more to help parents in the *barrio* understand what we were trying to do. Some of the parents had confidence in us but many were suspicious. They assumed that we must belong to one of the armed groups, or else they thought that the work-shops were useless. I made arrangements to speak about our work at a local community meeting, but I received a warning that I shouldn't go. I was told it might be dangerous. Then someone called me at home and told me to leave the *barrio* or they would kill me.

I said, "But I have done nothing bad."

The person said, "You have to go, or we will have to kill you."

They phoned my school and said the same thing. I spoke with people in the church and at UNICEF and none of us were sure if the threats were real. People often make threats in Colombia but they don't always carry them out. I was afraid though, so I went to Medellín for a while to stay with my sister.

I didn't like it there. We were living in a very rough and poor part of the city. I felt alienated and lonely. I kept thinking, "Why do I have to be displaced?" There was no reason for it. I had done nothing to deserve it. I was bored out of my mind since I had nothing to do. My mother also suffered while I was away — that was another reason why I wanted to go back. Eventually I called some people I knew in one of the armed groups. They asked some questions and then they told me, "No, you have no problem here in Apartadó."

I went back home but then I received another threat. I was very afraid. I couldn't sleep. I cried at night because I felt so insecure. For a while I stopped doing the workshops and stayed at home, but that made me even more miserable. After a few months I started working with the children again. I couldn't stay away.

I was raised in a violent environment but I didn't choose that path. I used to think that in order to survive, you had to have a weapon in your hands. Now I know that what we really need are positive ideas. If you think positively about yourself and others then you can make a good life, and build a good community.

I've changed a lot because of my involvement in the peace movement. First I changed because of the work, then because other people began to see me in a different way. I learned that my ability to dance, to have fun, and to be happy is a real gift that I can share and use to help other people. I learned that the abuse of the rights of children lies behind all their tragedies. I came to see my own journey through childhood as a struggle against the abuse of my own rights — including the right not to be recruited as a child soldier, the right to be protected from violence, and the right not to work underage. I know that I have been saved from my own "drowning" by having my right to participate respected.

I have learned also that there are many different ways of making peace. Every child we help, every volunteer we recruit, that is someone who can help us build a better community, a better country. Making peace isn't just about talking — it is about taking action.

# where are we now?

THE **CHILDREN'S MOVEMENT FOR PEACE** NOW HAS MORE than 100,000 active members. Many come into the Movement through the church, the Colombian Scouts, the Colombian Red Cross, Redepaz, YMCA, World Vision, and other organizations. But anyone under the age of eighteen, doing anything to help improve the quality of life in a community affected by violence, is considered an automatic member of the Movement. In Spring 2000, newspaper advertisements invited children and teenagers across the country to sign on with the Movement and describe their activities for peace. It drew tens of thousands of replies.

Most members interviewed for *Out of War* said that the biggest problem facing the Movement is lack of communication. Most are without easy access to telephones and computers, so they have to depend on adults to keep them informed about activities of the Movement in other parts of the country.

After his father was murdered, JUAN ELIAS and his family

continued to receive threats. In 1997 these became so intense that they decided to leave Aguachica and try to begin a new life in a new town. But the threats continued. They have been forced to move several times since, always suddenly and in secret. Juan Elias would like to study law and human rights at a university but the current circumstances of his family have made this difficult. He insists that no matter what happens, he will continue working for peace.

In August 2000, Luis Fernando Rincón, the former mayor of Aguachica, who helped to inspire Juan Elias to work for peace, was assassinated.

FARLIS, the outspoken daughter of a banana plantation worker, became a powerful spokesperson for the Children's Movement for Peace. Until she turned eighteen in 1999 she was its most visible representative. Farlis traveled to many countries, addressing audiences that sometimes numbered in the thousands, and occasionally included presidents and Nobel laureates.

Everywhere she has told the stories of the Children's and Citizen's Mandates, explaining that "at certain times, when countries fall into very great difficulties, children can hold the key to the future." She has talked about the meaning of peace for children, and how having peace at home and in the community is just as important as making peace in the war.

Farlis graduated from high school and for a while was uncertain if she would be able to fulfill her dream of going to college. In 1999, Colombia's prestigious University of the Andes awarded her a scholarship. She is now studying psychology in Bogotá and hopes to work in the rehabilitation of former child soldiers and other children traumatized by war.

For the other young people whose stories are told in this book, life remains much the same. "ALBERTO" continues to wait for the return of his brother. "We have just passed the second anniversary of the kidnapping." MARITZA sometimes takes part in peace workshops, but her life at home remains as difficult as ever. "I still walk two paths. I don't know which one will win."

HERMINSUL is much happier working in the Plaza de Flores without the perpetual threat of violence from the "vultures," but is always on the look-out for new opportunities.

The work of WILFRIDO, JOHEMIR, and other volunteers in the Return to Happiness program received special recognition from the Women's Commission for Refugee Women and Children in 1999. The Commission honored the Movement with its "Voices of Courage" award for its services to displaced families.

MAYERLY, WILFRIDO, BETO, and JOHEMIR would love to be able to go to college but their opportunities are limited by lack of funds. WILFRIDO'S ambition is to "live and work in Africa with other children affected by war. I wish I could share my experience with young people there." BETO would also like to work with children in a poorer country. JOHEMIR feels trapped by poverty. He is afraid that when he graduates from high school next year he will be forced to enter the army. "No one in my country can refuse to fight as a matter of conscience."

MAYERLY would like to study international relations and to become a leader. She said, "I believe that children are instruments of peace but it is hard for adults to clear their minds and really hear us. Many of them think we have no business talking about serious issues like the war, yet we cannot avoid the problems they have created for us. We have to be involved in the solution — or else the war and the violence will continue.

"Children are already doing a lot to improve our country.

We have helped to make peace the most important political topic for our nation. We have convinced the government that they should not recruit anyone under eighteen into the armed forces. We are building unity among young people from all over Colombia that never existed before. We are spreading the idea of children as peacemakers in schools and communities in many parts of Colombia, and even beyond.

"Children are the seeds of peace; we are the seeds that will stop the war."

# author's note

IN APRIL 1998, I WAS INVITED TO COLOMBIA BY CECILIO Adorna, who ran the UNICEF office in Bogotá. He wanted me to research and write a report on the Children's Movement for Peace because the Movement had been nominated for a Nobel Peace Prize. The report I wrote was to be sent to the Nobel Committee in Oslo, Norway.

Cecilio and Nidya Quiroz, who also worked with UNICEF, were influential supporters of the Movement, but I was free to do my own investigation and reach my own conclusions. At first I was skeptical. I didn't believe that children could do anything substantial to help peace. But during April 1998 and a second visit in July of the same year, I interviewed more than 150 children and teenagers who were all connected with the Movement. Sometimes I met with groups of five or ten; more often there were just one or two. Often I asked hard questions but the answers were always delivered with amazing composure, even if they were painful. I saw that children who had known violence, but had chosen peace, possessed insights that went far beyond their years.

Yet the Movement was confusing. I interviewed more than fifty adults from various organizations, who all seemed to have different ideas about what the Children's Movement had become — and these were different again from the young people who actually belonged to it. Some adults thought that the Movement was no longer significant. A lot of Colombians, adults and children, had never heard of it. Yet the Movement was real and was doing important work.

I spent most of the summer of 1998 in New York writing my report "Making Peace With Children." Often I wept, not just because of the tragedy of Colombia and the courage of the young people I had met, but because I felt an obligation to them. When they told me their stories it was as if they had placed something precious in my hands. I didn't feel that writing a report would be enough. I also believed that the ideas behind the Children's Movement for Peace were important, not just for Colombia, but for children everywhere who had to live with violence.

After completing the report, I continued writing articles,

sending e-mails, and telling anyone who would listen about the Movement. Those efforts helped to prompt film producer Kathy Eldon to make the CNN documentary *Soldiers of Peace: A Children's Crusade*. I went back to Colombia in May 1999 as a consultant during the filming. With UNICEF support I was able to visit Colombia again in 2000 and to continue working on the book throughout that year. Marina Curtis-Evans, a British woman living in Bogotá, became my interpreter, researcher, and a lifeline for me to the young people in the Movement after I returned to New York.

Since 1998, I have interviewed hundreds of wonderful young Colombians whose stories could not be told here because of insufficient space. Those interviews ran like conversations that occasionally dived into detail. I asked about the weather on a particular day, the size and look of a room, the atmosphere of a street, the way the light fell, how a teacher looked or spoke. I asked about dreams and secret friends and what could be seen from a particular doorway or window. I gradually learned more Spanish, but never enough to work without an interpreter. Marina's special empathy was a bonus, and sometimes she threw in questions of her own. The slower pace of working with an interpreter was also helpful because there was time to think and feel and construct the story as we went along.

Using their real words to guide the narrative, I wrote the stories in New York, then sent them back to Marina in Bogotá. She translated them into Spanish and sent them on to Wilfrido, Beto, and the others so that final corrections could be made.

Telling the stories of these remarkable young people has been a revelation for me. The most important and humbling lesson was that no matter how cleverly I could analyze the role of the Movement, their own voices were much more powerful than my own in explaining it. I learned to hold back, to make way for what they were trying to say, and to accept my role as that of an amplifier.

As a footnote, many of the adults I interviewed expressed concern that members of the Children's Movement for Peace would become disillusioned by the slowness or even the failure of the peace talks. Despite major concessions by the government negotiators, massacres and assassinations have continued, kidnappings have increased, and so have the number of families forced to abandon their homes. Threats against human rights activists have continued and many have been forced into exile. Unofficial emigration has also soared.

Yet fears that members of the Children's Movement would be disillusioned and give up the struggle for peace seem unfounded. Many of the adults I spoke to seemed far more impatient for peace, and more skeptical.

Farlis told me, "My generation is the one that will make the peace, but we won't get to enjoy it for a long time. The babies that are being born today, they are the ones who will know what peace means."

Mayerly said, "Of course we want to have peace immediately, but just because it doesn't come that isn't a reason to give up. If you give up on peace, how will you ever achieve it?"

# resources

YOU CAN LEARN MORE ABOUT THE CHILDREN'S MOVEMENT FOR PEACE AT
THE FOLLOWING WEB SITES:

www.unicef.org    The web site for the United Nations Children's Fund
(UNICEF). In addition to learning more about the Children's Movement for Peace, you can read about other
young people who are affected by war and violence. You
can also log on to Voices of Youth and share your
thoughts with young people from all over the world.

www.turnerlearning.com/cnn/soldiers

Supports the film *Soldiers of Peace: A Children's Crusade.* It also
contains a lot of good information about Colombia and
the Children's Movement for Peace. Teachers who are interested in obtaining a copy of the film for use in the
classroom may write to saracameron@outofwar.org.

www.worldvision.org

The web site for World Vision. Click on *Search* and type
in Children's Movement for Peace. You'll find articles and
a video featuring Mayerly.

http://www.geocities.com/EnchantedForest/Creek/8238/index.htm

The official web site of the Children's Movement for
Peace; it's in Spanish. If you can't read Spanish, you can
look at the photographs. Click on *Imágenes del Movimiento*
(which means "Images of the Movement") and you'll find
some surprises. (Hint: click on *siguiente* to get to the next
photo.)

http://www.latino.com/article.phtml/000414pazc

This web site has several interesting articles about the
Children's Movement for Peace. It is also available in
Spanish.

## USEFUL ADDRESSES

THE FOLLOWING ORGANIZATIONS SUPPORT THE CHILDREN'S MOVEMENT FOR PEACE AND CAN PROVIDE ADDITIONAL INFORMATION.

UNICEF Headquarters
3 UN Plaza
New York, NY 10017 USA
Telephone: 212-326-7000

Cruz Roja Colombiana
(The Red Cross of Colombia)
Youth Division
Cra. 68 No. 66-31
Santafé de Bogotá
Colombia

Profamilia Youth Center
Cra. 15 No. 34-47
Santafé de Bogotá
Colombia

Visión Mundial (World Vision)
Calle 13 No. 6-82
Santafé de Bogotá
Colombia

Citizens Mandate for Peace
Cra. B No. 90-0-2 Torre B Apto 202
Santafé de Bogotá
Colombia

Peace School for Youth
Abraham Lincoln High School
Diagonal 170 No. 59-57
Bachillerato
Santafé de Bogotá
Colombia

YMCA
Cra. 16A No. 28-33
Santafé de Bogotá
Colombia

UNICEF Bogotá
Transversal 38 No. 100-25 Piso 3
Santafé de Bogotá
Colombia
Telephone: 57 1 635 7066

Society of Jesuits
Programme for Peace
Calle 35 No. 21-19
Santafé de Bogotá
Colombia

Rafael Pombo Foundation
Calle 10 No. 5-22
Santafé de Bogotá
Colombia

The Scouts of Colombia
(Boys and Girls)
Calle 34 No. 25-69
Santafé de Bogotá
Colombia

Redepaz
(The Peace Network)
Cra. 20 No. 37-21
Santafé de Bogotá
Colombia

Hermanitas de la Anunciación
Calle 40 No. 78A-84
Santafé de Bogotá
Colombia

Fundación Pais Libre
(Free Country Foundation)
Calle 72 No. 8-21 Int. 1
Santafé de Bogotá
Colombia

Christian Children's Fund
Tr. 27 39A-30
Santafé de Bogotá
Colombia

High Commissioner for Peace
The President's Office
Government of Colombia
Calle 7 No. 6-54
Santafé de Bogotá
Colombia

# acknowledgments

THE CHILDREN'S MOVEMENT FOR PEACE IS AN ORGANIZA-tion of young people, but it would have had far less impact without the vision of Cecilio Adorna and Nidya Quiroz of UNICEF, and Ana Teresa Bernal from the Redepaz peace network. They took risks and dedicated the resources that allowed the Movement to grow.

Most of us would know little of the Children's Movement for Peace if José Ramos Horta had not had the imagination and courage to nominate it for a Nobel Peace Prize. José has nominated the Movement four times since 1998 and says he will continue to do so "until they win."

The Children's Movement for Peace would not exist without the hard work of thousands of young people. Many thanks to all those who shared their lives and dreams so that this book could be written. Many more stories remain to be told. Special thanks to Dilia from Redepaz; to Gloria, Iván Darío, and Gabriel of the Scouts in Bogotá; to Erika Vanessa, Victoria, Paula Marcela, and other scouts of Caquetá; to Camila and other Scouts of Cali; to Marta, Monica, Diego, and other children from World Vision; to Erika, Lelis Isabel, and others at Benposta; to Javier, Camilo Andrés, and other students at the Colegio de San Bartolomé; to Cristian Camilo at the Fundación Rafael Pombo; to Juan Carlos, Lina María, and others at the Colombian Red Cross; to Alexander, Tani, Diana, and others in Urabá; to Linia and other *semilleros* in Medellín; to Judy, Jhon Fredy, and others in the peace program of San Cristóbal; to Juan Carlos, Andrea, and others of the YMCA in Bogotá; to Jairo, Carmen, and others at the Talleres de Vida; to Leidy Diana of the Organización Pro Niña Indefensa; to Jhon, the stilt walker, Paolo, and others in Armenia; to Nicolas, Natalia, and others from the Escuelas de Paz; to Angela, Sandra, Julio, Miguel Angel, and others of the Phoenix program in Medellín; to Paola, Beatriz Elena, María del Carmen, and others at the Mama Margarita Institute in Medellín; to César, Juan David, Tomás, Juan Daniel, and others in Cali; to Alex, María Alejandra and others in Carambolas; to Daicy, Daniela, and others at the Arzobispo García School in Medellín and to Alexander, Fabián, and others from Corabastos Market. Thanks also to all the other children who participated in the workshops in Bogotá, Medellín, Cali, Apartadó, Turbo, Florencia-Caquetá, Florida Blanca, and Bucaramanga.

I cannot express enough thanks to Cecilio Adorna and Nidya Quiroz for bringing me to Colombia. I am profoundly grateful to Patricia Lone, Chief of Publications at UNICEF Headquarters, who gave the book creative space, time, and endless encouragement. Carel de Rooy and Clara Marcela Barona from UNICEF Colombia gave me accommodation, advice, support and, most precious of all, their friendship. Many other UNICEF staff gave valuable support, especially Marjorie Newman Williams, Bill Hetzer, Ruth Landy, Ellen Tolmie, Jeanette Gonzalez, Encke King, Loch Phillips, Margaret Kyenkya Isabirye, César Romero, and Susana Sánchez.

I was continually amazed by the warmth and willingness of Colombians to explain their much-misunderstood country. I am grateful to Ana Teresa Bernal, Diego Luis Arias, and others of Redepaz; "Pacho" Santos of El Tiempo; Antanas Mockus, now Mayor of Bogotá; Augusto Ramírez Ocampo, now Minister for Development; Héctor Fabio Henao and Alberto Maldonaldo of the Conferencia Episcopal; Leomidas Moremo, Pilar Plaza Queralt, Hildemaro Cruz, and others in Urabá; Carlos Castellanos of CINEP; Leonidas Manuel López of the Corporación Regiónal in Medellín; John Fernando Mesa of the University of Antioquia; Edith Cecilia Vega and others of the Colombian Red Cross; María Eugenia Ramírez and others of the Defense for Children International; Jorge Rojas of CODHES; Estella Duque Cuesta and Denis de Rojas of Talleres de Vida; José Luis Campos of Benposta; Clara Teresa Cárdenas de Arbelaez of Fundación Rafael Pombo; Oswaldo Ardila, Edgar Flores, and Rosalba Perez of World Vision; Pedro Patiño of Profamilia; Nydia Arguello, Myriam Orozco, and others at the YMCA; Luz Amanda Ortiz of Corporacíon Convivencia; Emilia Casas and others in the Colombian Scout Movement, including Javier Nieto in Cali and Oscar Gutierrez Agudelo and others in Caquetá.

Thanks also to Ambassador Alfonso Valdivieso and Ambassador Andrés Franco of the Permanent Mission of Colombia to the United Nations; Hernando Ramos and others of the Phoenix Program in Medellín; Sister Martha Isabel Minotta of the Hermanitas de la Asunción; Fabiola Ochoa of the Mama Margarita Institute; Martha Isabel Quintero from the Casa de Juventud, Armenia; Amada Benavides of the Escuelas de Paz; Fernando Cardona at the Colegio Bello Oriente, Carambolas; Franklin Daza and David Macías Scarpeta of the Colegio Iván Darío López, Cali; María Auxilio Gallo of the Arzobispo García School in Medellín; Juan Barbero, Jorge Camacho, Otty Patiño, León Valencia, and Francisco Ortíz.

Kathy Eldon, Amy Eldon, Kyra Thompson, Lydia Smith, and others made *Soldiers of Peace* into a powerful and inspirational documentary.

I am grateful and indebted to the enthusiasm, dedication, commitment, and empathy of Marina Curtis-Evans, as well as her skill with both languages.

Most of all love and thanks to my husband George McBean and our children, Fergus, Ainslie, and Ramsay — who always "understand."

I have done my best to tell these stories truthfully. Any faults are my own.